FIQH OF MENSTRUATION SIMPLIFIED

A Beginner's Guide for Muslim Women

NAIELAH ACKBARALI

Fiqh of Menstruation Simplified
A Beginner's Guide for Muslim Women

Author Email: help@muslimacoaching.com

ISBN: 978-1-7395999-2-8 *Paperback*

Published in England by
Inspired Muslim Women Ltd
Romford, United Kingdom
Tel: +44 7 915 765 815
Email: info@inspiredmuslimwomen.com
Website: www.inspiredmuslimwomen.com

British Library Cataloguing in Publication Data.
A catalogue record for this book is also available from the British Library.

بِسْمِ اللهِ الرَّحْمَنِ الرَّحِيم

To every sister,
who helped me,
guided me,
or inspired me.
Thank you.

Transliteration Table

ARABIC LETTER	ENGLISH TRANSLITERATION	ARABIC LETTER	ENGLISH TRANSLITERATION
ء	’	ض	ḍ
ا	a, ā	ط	ṭ
ب	b	ظ	ẓ
ت	t	ع	ʿ, ʿa, ʿi, ʿu
ث	th	غ	gh
ج	j	ف	f
ح	ḥ	ق	q
خ	kh	ك	k
د	d	ل	l
ذ	dh	م	m
ر	r	ن	n
ز	z	و	w, ū, u
س	s	ه	h
ش	sh	ي	y, ī, i
ص	ṣ		

ARABIC SYMBOL	ENGLISH TRANSLITERATION	ENGLISH TRANSLATION
ﷺ	*ṣalla ’Llāhu ʿalayhi wa sallam*	Allāh bless him and give him peace.
عليه السلام	*ʿalahī as-salām*	Peace be upon him.
رضي الله عنهم	*raḍiya ’Llāhu ʿanhum*	May Allāh be pleased with them.
رضي الله عنها	*raḍiya ’Llāhu ʿanhā*	May Allāh be pleased with her.
رضي الله عنه	*raḍiya ’Llāhu ʿanhu*	May Allāh be pleased with him.

Contents

Introduction

"Indeed, We created humans in the best form."

(*at-Tīn*, 95:4)

Allah Most High is the best of Creators. He fashioned women to menstruate, and through this blessing they can possibly give birth to children and be honored with continuing the lifeline of this *ummah*. The journey of menstruation itself is a progression of physical stages that facilitate the noble act of childbearing.

When a woman first reaches puberty, menstrual blood makes an abrupt entrance into her life. A young girl could be met with the challenges of hormonal fluctuations and physical development. She may experience tiredness, mood swings, headaches, and pelvic pain – possibly as a preparation for the road of responsibility that lies ahead.

As she enters the childbearing years of her twenties and thirties, her cycles may become more regular and routine, or they may never settle into an expected pattern, which can present challenges for some.

Once she approaches her forties and fifties, her body will undergo another stage of transformation as she welcomes the end of her period woes with menopause.

A woman's aging process is like a blossoming flower. She starts as a seed that roots herself into the ground. As time passes, she grows into a stem and begins to bud. Flower petals eventually appear as she matures and blooms, which beautify her unique shape, color, and size. Then, as the seasons pass, the petals begin to fall away until she returns to her Creator for the ultimate stage of her existence.

What is evident from this cycle is that women will spend a large portion of their lives menstruating. Thus, it is imperative for women to understand what Allah Most High wants from them in the various circumstances that they face.

This guide is a simplified version of the *fiqh* of menstruation. It is intended to help women who are beginning to learn this essential knowledge. More explanation and details can be found in our intermediate guide 'A Muslim Woman's Guide to Menstruation Rulings.'

By sticking to the basics, the hope is that it will provide a foundation for growth in understanding, developing, and blossoming in the Islamic rulings that Allah Most High has willed for women to follow.

PART 1

THE ISLAMIC PERSPECTIVE

Allah Says...

Today I have perfected your religion for you and have completed My favor upon you and chosen Islam as the way for you.

(*al-Mā'ida,* 5:3)

Say (O Prophet): "If you really love Allāh, then follow me, and Allāh shall love you and forgive your sins. Allāh is Most-Forgiving, Most-Merciful.

(*Āli 'Imrān*, 3:31)

They ask you about menstruation. Say: "It is an impurity. So, keep away from women during menstruation, and do not have intercourse with them until they are purified. When they purify themselves, then you may approach them in the manner specified by Allah. Verily Allāh loves those who always turn to Him in repentance and those who purify themselves.

(*al-Baqara*, 2:222)

1. Aisha's Hajj

It was the tenth year after the *hijra*, the last year of the Prophet Muḥammad's ﷺ life. Yet, no one knew that his ﷺ demise was to come. The Prophet ﷺ intended to undertake *ḥajj* during this year. It was the only *ḥajj* that the Prophet ﷺ performed after it became compulsory. Less than three months later, he ﷺ would suddenly fall sick and pass away.

Thousands of the Companions رضي الله عنهم came from various parts of the Arabian Peninsula to complete the *ḥajj* with the Prophet ﷺ. As for his wives رضي الله عنهن, all of them accompanied him to Makkah during his final pilgrimage.

The Prophet ﷺ and his Companions رضي الله عنهم left Madīna when there were only five days remaining of the month of *Dhū'l Qa'da*. They entered into a state of pilgrim sanctity (*iḥrām*) just a few miles outside of Madīna at Dhūl Ḥulayfah, which is known as Masjid ash-Shajara in today's times.

The Prophet ﷺ ordered those with him to intend what they wanted. There are different intentions that a pilgrim can make for *ḥajj*. A pilgrim can intend to do *ḥajj* only (*ifrād*), or a *ḥajj* and an *'umra* together with the same intention (*qirān*), or an *'umra* by itself and a *ḥajj* by itself (*tamattu'*). The Prophet's ﷺ beloved wife Lady 'Ā'isha رضي الله عنها intended to do the latter type, which is an *'umra* and a *ḥajj* with separate intentions.

The Companions رضي الله عنهم were so excited to perform the *ḥajj*. They chanted the *talbiya* throughout their trip down to Makkah. One can only dream of how elated their spirits were and the immense honor that they must have felt to be part of the Prophet's pilgrimage ﷺ.

The Prophet ﷺ and his Companions ﷺ entered Makkah on the fourth of *Dhū'l Ḥijjah*, prepared to complete the sacred rites due upon them. However, Lady ʿĀ'isha ﷺ started to menstruate before that at Sarif, a location that is approximately ten miles outside of Makkah.

She was already in the state of pilgrim sanctity, and not knowing what was to come, she became deeply saddened by the thought that she could not do *ḥajj* at all.

In her own narration, she describes what happened and says:

> "We set out with the Prophet ﷺ for *ḥajj*, and we were not making mention of anything except *ḥajj*. When we reached Sarif, I got my menses. When the Prophet ﷺ came to me, I was crying. He ﷺ asked, 'Why are you weeping?' I said, 'I wish – by Allāh! - that I had not performed *ḥajj* this year.' He asked, 'Perhaps you got your menses?' I replied, 'Yes.' He then said, '**This is a thing which Allāh has written for the daughters of Adam**. So do what all the pilgrims do except that you do not perform the *ṭawāf* around the Kaʿba until you are (ritually) pure.'"
>
> (*Bukhārī*, 305)

Lady ʿĀ'isha ﷺ was crying out of disappointment. She did not want to miss the momentous experience of *ḥajj*, but what could she do? In those days, there were no hormonal medications that existed to stop her menstrual flow.

She had to submit to Allāh Most High's will, but it was nevertheless a heartbreaking moment for her – even to the extent that she wished that she had not performed *ḥajj* that year! Little did she know that this would be the only *ḥajj* that her beloved husband ﷺ would perform, and he ﷺ would die only a few months later in her own arms.

The Prophet's ﷺ response to Lady ʿĀ'isha's crying was exemplary in many ways. Firstly, he ﷺ knew why she was crying. This is the type of loving relationship that they had with each other. He ﷺ could sense his wife's emotional state.

Secondly, he was gentle in his approach. He ﷺ saw that she was in pain and reached out to her in a caring way. His words comforted and consoled her worries. And what were his words? That women are the daughters of Prophet Adam ﷺ.

Sometimes people think that menstruation is dirty and disgusting, but the Prophet ﷺ elevated women to the lofty status of being the progeny of the first Prophet to mankind because of their monthly cycles.

This *ḥadīth* also proves that menstruation is not a punishment. Rather, menstruation is natural and normal – something which Allāh Most High has ordained for all women until the end of time.

In fact, Allāh Most High honored women with their monthly cycles. If it were not for menstruation, Muslim women could not get pregnant, have children, and continue to uphold the lifeline of the *ummah*.

The Prophet ﷺ informed Lady ʿĀ'isha ﷺ that she could perform *ḥajj*, but she could not do the *ṭawāf*. This is the only *ḥajj* ritual that a menstruating women must avoid until her menstruation ceases.

She can do everything else: camp at Minā, stand at ʿArafat, sleep at Muzdalifa, stone the *jamarāt*, carry out the slaughtering, make *dhikr*, supplicate, engage in repentance, make *ṣalawāt*, and much more.

Lady ʿĀʾisha ﵂ followed through with the Prophetic instruction. She exited her pilgrim state for *ʿumra* and entered into a new pilgrim state for *ḥajj*. She completed the standing at ʿArafat, and when her menstruation ended she performed the *ṭawāf* on *ʿĪd* day.

She accepted that this is what Allāh Most High had willed for her. Furthermore, she was still able to benefit and have a spiritual experience despite her circumstance.

In another narration, Lady ʿĀʾisha ﵂ told the Prophet ﷺ that everyone else had completed a *ḥajj* and an *ʿumra* but she had only done a *ḥajj*. The Prophet ﷺ ordered her brother, ʿAbdur Raḥmān ibn Abī Bakr ﵄, to take her to Tanʿīm so that she could enter into a state of pilgrim sanctity for *ʿumra*. (*Muslim*, 1213)

In today's times, this location is demarcated by a mosque known as Masjid ʿĀʾisha. It is where everyone goes nowadays to enter into pilgrim sanctity (*iḥrām*) for *ʿumra* once they are in Makkah.

Because of Lady ʿĀʾisha's situation ﵂, Muslim women know what to do when they experience menstruation during *ḥajj*. More than this, all Muslims know where to go if they want to perform another *ʿumra*. Her trial, her pain, and her worry over her menstruation became a symbol of Islam – landmarked by a *masjid* that people will use until the end of time.

2. The Right Mindset

"But perhaps you hate a thing and it is good for you; and perhaps you love a thing and it is bad for you. And Allāh Knows, while you know not."

(al-Baqara, 2:216)

It is quite common for women to complain about their period woes. The cramping, the headaches, and the messy bleeding on a monthly basis could be viewed as inconvenient.

However, believing women must overlook the emotional highs and lows of their menstrual cycle and direct their focus upon what the religion of Islam says about menstruation.

Islam does not consider menstruation to be a punishment. Quite the contrary, menstruation is viewed as a natural and normal process that healthy women experience throughout their lifetime.

A menstruating woman is not dirty, but rather from a legal perspective she is ritually impure for the duration that she is menstruating. This classification has legal consequences and not spiritual consequences.

As such, a menstruating woman is instructed by Allāh Most High to stop certain forms of worship, and every second that she obeys these commands, it is worship if done for Allāh Most High's sake.

The rulings of menstruation have other benefits.

They make a woman aware of her body, so that she takes care of it.

They instill a longing for her to perform certain acts of worship, so she is keen to pray and fast once her bleeding ends.

They compel her to learn the Islamic sciences, so she increases in love for her religion.

They keep her conscious of her Lord's commands, so she is avid to obey His orders throughout her days and nights.

Menstruation is not a barrier to a woman's spirituality. Instead, it is an opportunity to learn how to devote herself to Allāh Most High in a different way. Following the rulings and living them out in her daily life is a means for reward.

Recommended Readings from the Appendix:

- How the Prophet ﷺ Treated Menstruating Women

3. Prohibitions & Permissions

According to the *Ḥanafī madhhab*, there are nine actions that a woman in a state of menstruation (*hayḍ*) or lochia (*nifās*) needs to avoid:

1. Performing the ritual prayer or prostrating.
2. Fasting.
3. Touching the Qur'ān.
4. Reciting the Qur'ān.
5. Entering any mosque.
6. Making *ṭawāf*.
7. Engaging in sexual intercourse.
8. Being directly touched between the navel to the knee.
9. Being divorced.

Sometimes it is hard to accept the list of dos and don'ts that apply to a menstruating woman. It is doubly difficult during *Ramaḍān* when everyone is fasting, and even more so during *'umra* and *ḥajj*. It is a common complaint from menstruating ladies that they feel left out.

Scholars unanimously agree that all Sacred Law rulings have a benefit in them, even if humans cannot rationally deduce it. Allāh Most High loves His creation, and He will always decree what is best for them.

It is true that during a woman's menstruation certain acts of worship cannot be performed. Yet, one must keep in mind that they are only a select number, and many more acts remain permissible. Allāh Most High is not closing the doors of worship during the time of menstruation.

Allah Most High says clearly says in the Qur᾽ān:

"I did not create the jinn and humans except to worship Me."

(al-Dhāriyāt, 51:56)

Furthermore, if a menstruating woman avoids certain actions with the intention to submit to Allāh Most High's command, she is actually worshiping Allāh the entire time that she refrains from these acts.

In the *Ḥanafī madhhab*, it is recommended that a menstruating woman make *wuḍū᾽* for each prayer time, sit in her usual place of worship, and make remembrance (*dhikr*) for the time it takes her to normally pray so that she does not lose her habit of worship.

◆ **She cannot pray the ritual prayer or fast, but she can:**

- Supplicate for whatever she wishes.
- Make remembrance (*dhikr*) of Allāh Most High.
- Make *ṣalawāt* on the Prophet ﷺ.

◆ **She cannot recite the Qur᾽ān or touch it, but she can:**

- Listen to the Qur᾽ān.
- Memorize Prophetic *du᾽ā᾽* and *ḥadīth*.
- Say Quranic *du᾽ā᾽* with the intention of supplication.

- ✧ Read the Qurʾān on a computer screen with her eyes only (no touching or producing sound).
- ✧ Touch the Qurʾān with a detached barrier, like a cloth.

◆ **She cannot enter a mosque or do *ṭawāf*, but she can:**

- ✧ Teach, study, and review sacred knowledge.
- ✧ Listen to religious lectures and read the *sīra*.
- ✧ Enter an Islamic center for classes and learn.
- ✧ Walk around the mosque courtyard in Madīna.

◆ **She cannot engage in sexual intercourse or be directly touched between the navel and knee, but she can:**

- ✧ Kiss, hug, and do other intimate acts over her leggings.
- ✧ Be sexually aroused and satisfied.
- ✧ Demonstrate good character towards her spouse.
- ✧ Emotionally connect with her spouse.

CONDITIONS FOR QURʾĀNIC SUPPLICATIONS

The menstruating woman's **intention** is to make *dhikr* or *duʿāʾ*, and it is not for reciting the Qurʾān.

The verses **contain** the meanings of *dhikr* or *duʿāʾ*, unlike verses that relate stories or legal rulings.

Examples of verses that she is **permitted** to say:

- ☑ *Sūrat'l-Ikhlāṣ*, *Sūrat'l-Falaq*, *Sūrat 'l-Nās*, and *Ayyat'l-Kursī* with the intention of seeking protection.
- ☑ *Sūrat'l-Fātiḥa* with the intention of making supplication.

MAKING UP MISSED PRAYERS:

A menstruating woman is not permitted to pray any type of prayer. Furthermore, she is not required to make up (*qaḍā'*) any of the prayers missed due to her menstruation.

For example, a woman menstruates for seven days. During this time, she is not permitted to perform the ritual prayer. After her menses ceases, she does not owe the seven days of missed prayers.

MENSTRUATION STARTS WHILE PRAYING:

If a woman's menstruation starts while she is praying, the prayer becomes invalid from a legal perspective, but she will be rewarded for her efforts. According to the *Ḥanafī madhhab*, she only needs to make up the prayer if it was a voluntary prayer (*sunna/nafl*).

MENSTRUATION STARTS BEFORE PRAYING:

If a woman's menstruation starts after the prayer time entered, but she has not performed the obligatory prayer (*farḍ*) yet, she does not need to make up the prayer after her menses finishes.

Chart 3.1 - Summary of Rulings

ACTION	OBLIGATORY PRAYER	SUNNA / NAFL PRAYER
Missed Prayers During Menses	No Makeup	No Makeup
Menses Starts While Praying	No Makeup	Makeup
Menses Starts Before Praying	No Makeup	No Makeup

MAKING UP MISSED FASTS:

A woman is not permitted to fast any type of fast (*Ramaḍān*, *sunna*, or *nafl*) while she menstruates.

Unlike the prayer, a menstruating woman is required to make up any obligatory fasts that she misses from the month of *Ramaḍān*. She makes them up after *Ramaḍān* is over during a time when she is not menstruating. For more details, refer to **Question 2** in Section 17.

Women should record the number of fasting days missed so that they do not forget how many fasts are owed.

Section 17

MENSTRUATION STARTS WHILE FASTING:

If a woman's menstruation begins at any time between *Fajr* to *Maghrib*, she must stop fasting. The fast for that day does not count. She is obliged to make up this fast after her menstruation ends. This ruling applies to any type of fast (*Ramaḍān*, *sunna*, or *nafl*).

BLEEDING STOPS DURING THE DAY IN RAMADAN:

If a woman's menstruation stops at any moment between *Fajr* to *Maghrib*, then she takes a *ghusl*, starts praying, and acts like a fasting person until the *Maghrib* time enters due to the sacredness of the month of *Ramaḍān*. This ruling only applies to *Ramaḍān*.

Chart 3.2 - Summary of Rulings

BLEEDING STARTS DURING THE DAY IN RAMAḌĀN	BLEEDING STOPS DURING THE DAY IN RAMAḌĀN
• Fasting is unlawful. • Eating is done discretely. • Make up the fast later.	• Take a *ghusl* and pray. • Refrain from food and drink. • Make up the fast later.

DIRECTLY TOUCHING THE QUR'AN:

It is not permitted for a menstruating woman to directly touch a verse of the Qur'ān or the *muṣḥaf* (Arabic Qur'ān), including its insides, its page margins, and its cover. This applies to a translation of the Qur'ān, even if there is no Arabic text within it.

TOUCHING THE QUR'AN WITH A BARRIER:

It is permissible for a menstruating woman to touch a verse of the Qur'ān or the *muṣḥaf* with a non-attached barrier. The non-attached barrier must be completely removable from the *muṣḥaf*. Examples of a non-attached barrier are a cloth, box, or bag.

As for touching phones, refer to **Question 3** in Section 17.

Section 17

READING WITHOUT TOUCHING:

If no touching or holding is involved, it is permissible to read the Qur'ān with one's eyes. For example, a menstruating woman can read the Qur'ān while sitting in front of a computer screen. There should not be any recitation or sound made while reading.

Chart 3.3 - Summary of Rulings

TOUCHING DIRECTLY	RULING
***Muṣḥaf* or Verse**	Impermissible
Translation of the Qur'ān	Impermissible
Books Of Sacred Knowledge	Permitted
***Du'ā'* and *Dhikr* Books**	Permitted
Reading With Eyes - No Touching	Permitted

RECITING THE QURAN:

It is not permitted for a menstruating woman to recite any part of the Qur'ān. The definition for reciting is to move the lips while producing sound, even if it be whispering to oneself.

This includes reciting for reward, like reciting *Sūrat al-Kahf* on Fridays or *Sūrat al-Mulk* at night. Likewise, reciting *Sūrat Yā Sīn* for the dead. Refer to **Question 4** in Section 17 for *tajwid* classes.

? Section 17

DU'A, SALAWAT, & DHIKR:

It is permissible for a menstruating woman to make Qur'ānic supplications (see page 13 for details), say supplications narrated from the *sunna*, recite *ṣalāwāt*, and engage in *dhikr*.

READING WITHOUT MAKING SOUND:

It is permissible for a menstruating woman to read the Qur'ān with her heart without making sound. She can also listen to the Qur'ān.

Chart 3.4 - Summary of Rulings

RECITING	RULING
Qur'ān With Lips & Sound	Impermissible
Qur'ān for Reward	Impermissible
Qur'ān for Deceased	Impermissible
Qur'ānic Supplications & Dhikr	Permitted
Prophetic Supplications, *Dhikr*, & *Ṣalāwāt*	Permitted
Reading Qur'ān With Heart Only	Permitted
Listening to Qur'ān	Permitted

ENTERING THE MOSQUE:

It is not permitted for a menstruating woman to enter a mosque (*masjid*), even to pass through it. If her menstruation starts while she is in the mosque, she must leave immediately.

Islamic centers are different than mosques. It is permitted for a menstruating woman to enter them. However, she must avoid entering the main prayer area (*muṣalla*) of the center because it could take the ruling of a mosque. She is permitted to attend lectures and programs if they are held in other rooms in the center.

Women should check with their local *imām* to find out whether they are entering a mosque or an Islamic center.

OTHER PERMITTED PLACES:

It is permitted to walk within the courtyards outside *al-Masjid al-Ḥarām* in Makkah and *al-Masjid al-Nabawī* in Madīna. However, it is not permitted to enter the mosques.

If the *ʿĪd* prayer is conducted outside the mosque, such as at a convention center or an open field, it is permitted to enter the prayer area during menstruation. Likewise, entering a graveyard is allowed.

Chart 3.5 - Summary of Rulings

ENTERING & REMAINING	RULING
Mosque	Impermissible
Islamic Center	Permitted
Mosque Courtyard	Permitted
***ʿĪd* Prayer Area**	Permitted
Graveyard	Permitted

MAKING TAWAF DURING MENSTRUATION:

It is not permitted for a menstruating woman to circumambulate (make *ṭawāf*) around the *Ka'ba*, regardless of whether the *ṭawāf* is obligatory (*farḍ*), mandatory (*wājib*), *sunna*, or voluntary (*nafl*).

If a woman's menstruation starts before she begins to make *ṭawāf*, then she must wait until her menstruation finishes and she takes a *ghusl*. Thereafter, she can enter the mosque and make *ṭawāf*. Refer to **Question 5** in Section 17 for acts of worship she can perform.

Section 17

SEXUAL INTERCOURSE DURING MENSTRUATION:

It is not permitted for a menstruating woman to engage in sexual intercourse. If both spouses willingly engage in this act, they must each repent and ask for Allāh Most High for forgiveness.

TOUCHING BETWEEN THE NAVEL AND KNEES:

It is not permitted for a husband to directly touch the skin between his wife's navel to knees during menstruation. This is the ruling regardless of whether sexual desire is present or not. The prohibited area begins just below her navel and ends just below her knees. The knees, backside, hips, and thighs are included.

It is permitted for her husband to touch the prohibited area over a barrier. For example, the wife places a sheet over this part of her body, or she wears leggings. As for skin-to-skin contact with other areas of her body, such as the chest, back, arms, and calves, it is permissible.

For more rulings related to the prohibitions and permissions, refer to "A Muslim Woman's Guide to Menstruation Rulings."

PART 2

GETTING STARTED

Key Terminology

- **Menstruation** (*ḥayḍ*) is the normal, healthy vaginal blood that a woman expels from her uterus when she does not get pregnant.

- **Lochia** (*nifās*) is the normal, healthy vaginal blood that a pregnant woman expels from her uterus after childbirth or after the miscarriage of a developed fetus.

- **Abnormal uterine bleeding** (*istiḥāḍa*) is any vaginal blood that is not considered menstruation or lochia.

- A **purity span** (*ṭuhr*) is a duration of time that must separate between a menstruation and menstruation, or a lochia and menstruation, or a lochia and a lochia.

- The **habit** (*ʿāda*) is the last sound menses, sound lochia, or sound purity span that a woman experienced.

- A **woman with a habit** *(muʿtāda)* is a woman who has previously experienced menstruation or lochia.

- The ***ghusl*** is a purificatory shower that removes the state of ritual impurity after menses or lochia ends.

4. Female Anatomy

ʿĀʾisha ﷺ narrates: "How excellent are the women of the Ansār! They did not allow shyness to prevent them from learning their religion."

(*Muslim*, 332; *Abū Dāwūd*, 316)

It is essential to be aware of a woman's basic anatomy to comprehend the definition of menstruation and the rulings related to it. There are eight **female-only** body parts that women should be aware of:

1. **The Uterus:** Also known as the womb. It is a hollow muscular organ that is responsible for the development of the embryo and fetus. Menstrual blood is the shedding of the uterine lining when a woman does not get pregnant.

2. **The Cervix:** Also known as the neck of the uterus. During menstruation, the cervix dilates to allow the passage of menstrual flow. During pregnancy, the cervix and its mucus plug protect the fetus from external pathogens.

3. **The Fallopian Tubes and Fimbriae:** A pair of 4-inch (10 cm) long narrow tubes located in the pelvis extending from the upper corners of the uterus to the ovaries.

4. **The Ovaries:** The ovaries produce the female sex hormones that control reproduction. They are where ova (egg cells) are stored, developed, and released during ovulation. The open

ends of the fallopian tubes rest just beyond the surface of the ovaries to transport ova to the uterus.

5 **The Vagina:** An elastic, muscular tube connecting the cervix of the uterus to the external female genitalia.

Diagram 4.1 - Internal Female Organs

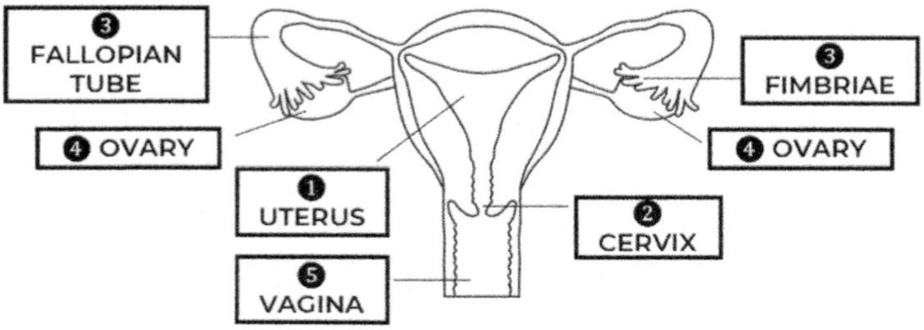

6 **The Labia Majora:** A pair of fleshy folds of skin and fatty tissue that are part of the external female genitalia (vulva).

7 **The Labia Minora:** A pair of thin folds that lie just inside the labia majora.

8 **The Clitoris:** The clitoris is made up of erectile tissue that contains thousands of nerve endings, which make it an extremely sensitive organ.

Diagram 4.2 - External Genital Structure

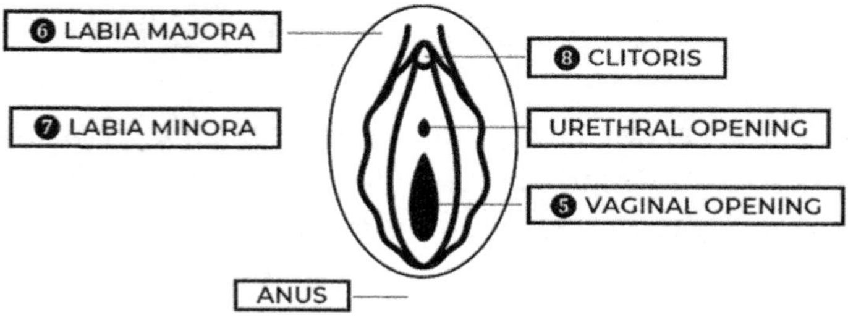

MENSTRUAL BLOOD:

Menstrual fluid contains a mixture of blood, cervical mucus, and cells from the lining of the uterus. According to doctors, a healthy menstrual flow resembles the color of cranberry juice. The bleeding lasts for 3 to 7 days, averaging 5 days.

It is normal to have heavier and lighter flow days. Heavier flow days usually occur at the beginning of a woman's menstruation, and the flow tends to lighten as the days go by. Expelling small clots of blood is also considered normal.

Diagram 4.3 - How the Menstrual Cycle Works

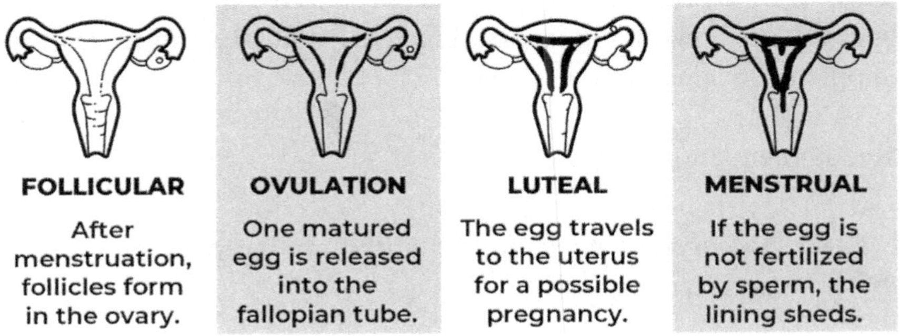
FOLLICULAR
After menstruation, follicles form in the ovary.
OVULATION
One matured egg is released into the fallopian tube.
LUTEAL
The egg travels to the uterus for a possible pregnancy.
MENSTRUAL
If the egg is not fertilized by sperm, the lining sheds.

THE MENSTRUAL CYCLE:

Medically-speaking, the menstrual cycle begins with the first day of a woman's period and ends just before her next period. A normal cycle lasts between 21 and 35 days. Each woman's cycle will differ.

NORMAL VAGINAL DISCHARGE:

Normal vaginal discharge is the discharge seen when a woman is not menstruating or in lochia. It is clear or white in color, and it may have a subtle scent that is not unpleasant or foul smelling.

PMS SYMPTOMS:

PMS (premenstrual syndrome) is the name for the physical and emotional symptoms that women can experience in the weeks before their period.

Common symptoms are cramps, headaches, acne, bloating, mood swings, breast tenderness, bloating, and diarrhea. Symptoms usually stop during or at the beginning of the menstrual period.

It is not fully understood why women get PMS, but it may be because of changes in their hormone levels during the menstrual cycle.

There is no cure for PMS, but symptoms may be managed successfully with lifestyle changes, dietary modifications, supplements, and other therapies.

Recommendations include:

Lifestyle: Exercising regularly, cutting back on caffeine, and sleeping more.

Dietary: Reducing salt intake and eating foods that provide calcium, such as yogurt, almonds, kale, and beans.

Supplements: Taking calcium, magnesium, evening primrose oil, chasteberry, and essential fatty acids can help reduce symptoms according to studies.

Therapies: Practicing mindfulness or breathing exercises may assist in reducing stress levels.

It is useful to keep a PMS diary and record any improvement in symptoms when trying out these suggestions.

DOCTORS VS TEACHERS:

Sometimes a conflict can arise between what is medically viewed as menstruation and what is Islamically viewed as menstruation.

For example, many doctors do not consider yellow to be a color of menstrual blood, but Islamically it is a color.

Another example is with the spotting of blood. Some doctors may not consider spotting to be menstruation, whereas Islamically it can be. Refer to **Question 10** in Section 17 for more details.

Section 17

When a conflict occurs between doctors and teachers:

Muslims must always act upon what the Sacred Law says with concerns related to the validity of their prayers, fasts, permissibility of sexual intercourse, and anything connected to the Islamic sphere of their lives.

The advice of doctors can be followed when their prognosis is used to determine if a person's body is physically healthy or if proper medical attention is needed to address a problem, such as abnormal bleeding or vaginal infections.

PART 3

MENSTRUATION MADE EASY

Menstruation Basics

DEFINITION

Menstruation (*ḥayḍ*) is:

Blood that originates from **the uterus** and exits out of the vagina of a female who is at least 9 lunar years old.

It is **not** blood due to an illness or injury.

It is **not** blood seen during pregnancy or after childbirth.

CONDITIONS

Its conditions are:

Its **minimum** duration is 3 complete days (72 hours).

Its **maximum** duration is 10 complete days (240 hours).

It must be **followed by** a purity span (*ṭuhr*) of at least 15 complete days (360 hours) free from any colored vaginal discharge.

RULING

If the blood abides by the definition and conditions of menstruation, the bleeding is ruled as sound, and it becomes the menses habit.

5. Menses Simplified

The Prophet ﷺ said, "The least menstruation can be is three days, and the most it can be is ten days."

(al-Ṭabarānī, Al-Muʿjam al-Kabīr, 7586)

Not every show of blood that a woman sees will be ruled as menstruation. There are actually three types of vaginal blood that a woman can experience: menstruation (*ḥayḍ*), lochia (*nifās*), and abnormal uterine bleeding (*istiḥāḍa*).

The way that a woman knows how to distinguish between the three types is by their definitions and conditions. If bleeding does not meet the definition or conditions of menstruation, then it is ruled as abnormal bleeding.

Menstruation is:

- **Blood:** This refers to all colored vaginal discharge that is not completely white or clear. It could be black, red, brown, yellow, or turbid in color.

  White or clear discharge that is mixed with a spot of color will take the ruling of blood too. Thus, a woman must not ignore any spotting that she sees.

  As for completely white or clear discharge, seeing it within the time of menstruation indicates that the bleeding has stopped. During the time of purity, its exiting may invalidate *wuḍūʾ*. Refer to **Question 9** in Section 17 for details.

? Section 17

- **Originates from the uterus:** This disqualifies blood that comes from urinary tract infections, anal fissures, and the like. The blood must come from the uterus.

- **Exits out of the vagina:** The bleeding must exit for the ruling of menstruation to come into effect. Therefore, if a woman feels cramps but blood does not exit the vagina, then she is not menstruating.

  The bleeding can exit naturally or when wiping the vagina with a tissue.

- **From a female who is at least 9 years old:** This phrase rules out younger girls who may see colored discharge. Nine lunar years is approximately 8 solar years and 9 months.

- **Not due to an illness:** Colored discharge that exits due to a confirmed vaginal infection is not menstruation.

- **Not due to injury:** Colored discharge that exits because of a confirmed injury – like the scraping of the cervix during a pap smear exam – is not menstruation.

- **Not seen during pregnancy:** Pregnant women cannot menstruate according to the *Ḥanafī* scholars, which is also in line with medical understanding.

- **Not seen after childbirth:** The vaginal blood seen after childbirth is called lochia (*nifās*).

There are three **additional conditions** to consider before a woman can confidently say that her bleeding is menstruation.

❶ The bleeding must reach a minimum of 3 complete days (72 hours), and it cannot be less than this duration.

What is intended by a 'day' is a full day and its night, which is 24 hours. Three days of 24 hours equals 72 hours.

Diagram 5.1 - Menstrual Minimum

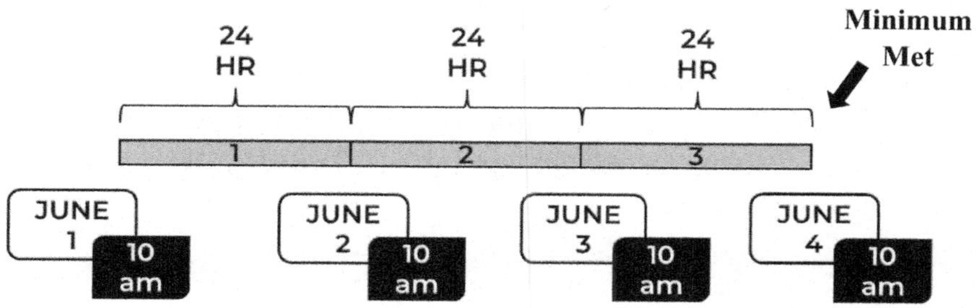

Furthermore, the bleeding can reach the menstrual minimum in the form of spotting, a light flow, or a full flow. There is no condition that it be constant or accompanied by physical symptoms like cramps.

Diagram 5.2 - Menstrual Minimum

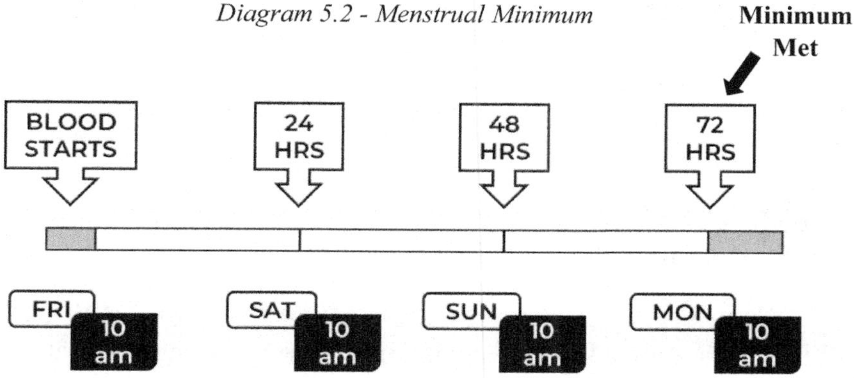

In Diagram 5.2, the entire duration from Friday 10 am to Monday 10 am is menstruation, even though the bleeding is not continuous.

2 It cannot exceed 10 complete days (240 hours).

A woman only has 10 days to menstruate. The blood during the 10 days can be any color and any type of flow.

Ten days of 24-hours is 240 hours, which is known as the menstrual maximum. Thereafter, menstruation can be no more. Any bleeding that exceeds the menstrual maximum of 10 days (240 hours) is ruled as abnormal bleeding.

Diagram 5.3 - Menstrual Maximum

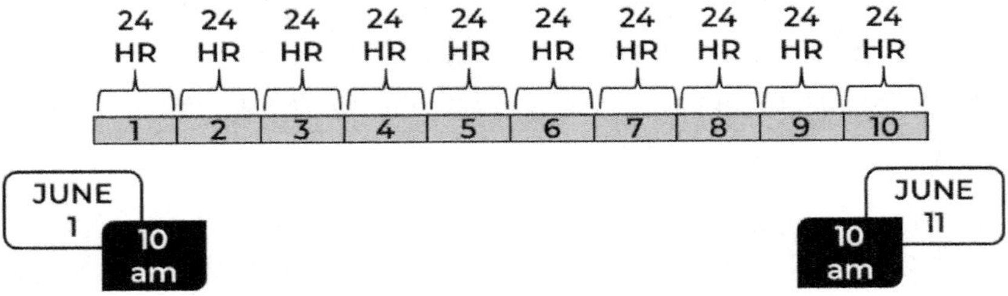

3 The bleeding must be followed by a purity span of 15 complete days (360 hours).

Fifteen days of 24-hours equals 360 hours. This purity span must also be free of colored discharge. Two menstruations cannot come back-to-back. There must always be a purity span that separates between them. Refer to Section 11 for details about purity spans.

If the blood abides by the definition and conditions of menstruation, the bleeding is ruled as sound, and it becomes a woman's menses habit.

THE HABIT:

A woman can have three habits: a menses habit, a lochia habit, and a purity habit.

It is obligatory upon every woman to record her habits. When abnormal bleeding occurs, the habit is used to determine which days are menstruation. The habit is also needed to know the rulings for other situations, like when it is permissible to engage in sexual intercourse after her *ghusl*.

A woman's menses habit is established with the most recent menses that she sees, providing that it fulfills the definition and conditions for menstruation. She only needs to see it occur once for the habit to be established.

Diagram 5.4 - Establishing A Menses Habit

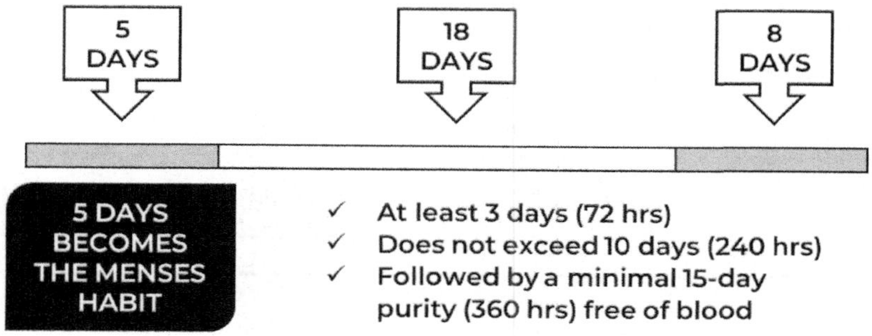

WOMEN MUST RECORD:

- ✧ The date and time any vaginal blood begins, including the spotting of blood.
- ✧ The date and time any vaginal blood ends.

Some women use a small notebook as a diary to record their dates. Others log their dates and times using an Excel sheet. By far, the most popular option is to use a period phone app due to its convenience.

However, it must be mentioned that phones are not always reliable. When they crash or get lost, it poses problems for women who urgently need to know their dates of bleeding. Therefore, it is best to create a backup copy and store it in a second place as a safeguard.

Women who never recorded their dates of bleeding should refer to the answer in **Question 1** in Section 17.

Section 17

Chart 5.5 - Sample Record

BLOOD STARTS	BLOOD ENDS	TOTAL DAYS OF BLOOD	TOTAL DAYS OF PURITY
January 5th 1 pm	*January 10th 2 pm + 15 mins GT (2:15pm)*	*5 days, 1 hour and 15 mins*	*22 days*
February 1st 2:15 pm	*February 8th 4 pm + 15 mins GT (4:15pm)*	*7 days and 2 hours*	*30 days, 4 hours and 45 mins*
March 10th 9 pm	*March 17th 10 pm + 15 mins GT (10:15pm)*	*7 days, 1 hour and 15 mins*	*22 days and 45 mins*
April 8th 11 pm	*April 12th 6 pm*	****Brown spots on April 25th 2 pm and April 27th 11 am*	

*GT refers to Ghusl Time, which is explained in Section 10.

6. Possible Days of Menses

"Allāh does not burden any soul with more than it can bear."

(*al-Baqara*, 2:286)

Allāh Most High is all-Merciful and He knows the limits of His creation. He revealed the Sacred Law as a comprehensive form of guidance to mankind. Menstruation rulings are part of that divine guidance, and they are a mercy to women.

The practical rulings of the Sacred Law direct a woman with how to act when her bleeding starts or stops so that she is not left questioning what to do.

The **rulings in the moment** are the daily guidelines that tell a woman how to move forward when her bleeding starts or stops, like whether she prays or fasts.

The **rulings in retrospect** are the retroactive rulings that come about when the details of a woman's circumstance change. They can overturn a ruling in the moment.

It is important to recognize this distinction when learning the rulings related to the possible days of menses.

The possible days of menses are the ten potential days that a woman could experience menstruation during the month. They start when a woman sees blood within her expected time of menstruation, which is usually known by the length of her purity habit. If she does not see blood after her purity habit finishes, then she keeps praying.

There are three main rulings related to the possible days:

1. **Whenever blood is seen within the possible days of menses, it is always considered menses.**

⇒ This includes any color of blood, like brown and turbid.

⇒ It also includes bleeding that is spotting, a light flow, or blood that stops and returns within the possible days.

⇒ A woman will not pray, fast, or engage in any of the prohibited acts while seeing blood in her possible days.

2. **Whenever blood stops before 3 complete days (72 hours) within the possible days, it is ruled as abnormal bleeding (*istiḥāḍa*), and she is obliged to make *wuḍū*ʾ and pray.**

⇒ This is when she knows that the blood will not return. Thus, this ruling may be more relevant to those who experience spotting instead of a consistent flow.

⇒ She starts praying since she is no longer seeing blood.

⇒ Because the bleeding did not meet the menstrual minimum of 3 days (72 hours), she only makes *wuḍū*ʾ and not *ghusl*. She also makes up any prayers missed for that duration.

Diagram 6.1 - Comparison of Before & After 72 Hours

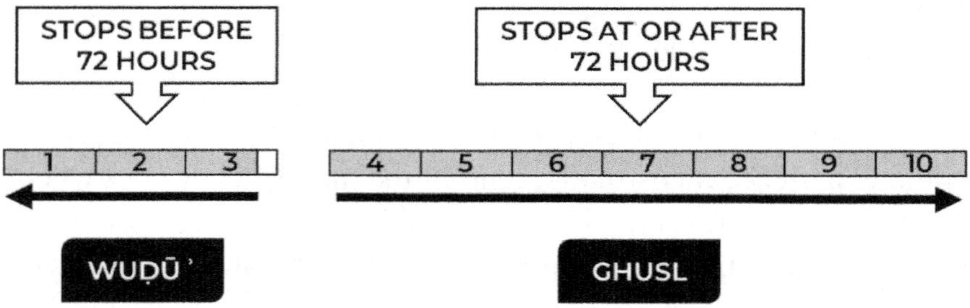

3 Whenever blood stops at 3 complete days (72 hours) or more within the possible days, it is ruled as menstruation (*ḥayḍ*), and she is obliged to take a *ghusl* and pray.

⇒ The sign that the bleeding has stopped is that she sees clear, white, or no discharge – and she is certain that the blood will not return.

⇒ She must take a *ghusl* before praying.

⇒ She is not required to make up any prayers missed during menstruation, but she must make up her *Ramaḍān* fasts.

⇒ If blood returns within the possible days, it is menses and she takes another *ghusl* when the blood stops. The worship performed in-between the two shows of blood is invalid and these days become menstruation in retrospect.

✔ If the entire span of bleeding does not exceed the menstrual maximum of 240 hours, then it becomes her new menses habit – providing that a purity span of 15 complete days free of blood follows it.

In Diagram 6.2, a woman sees bleeding after her purity habit of 30 days is finished. She stops praying and considers the bleeding to be menstruation. When the bleeding stops on Day 5, she takes a *ghusl* and begins to pray.

Diagram 6.2 - Possible Days of Menses

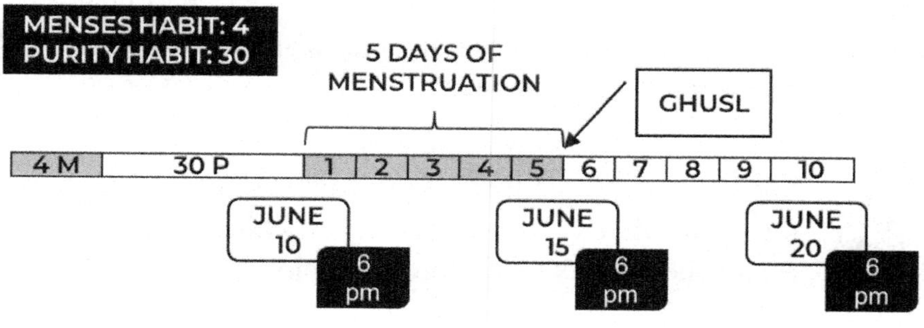

Diagram 6.3 - Possible Days of Menses

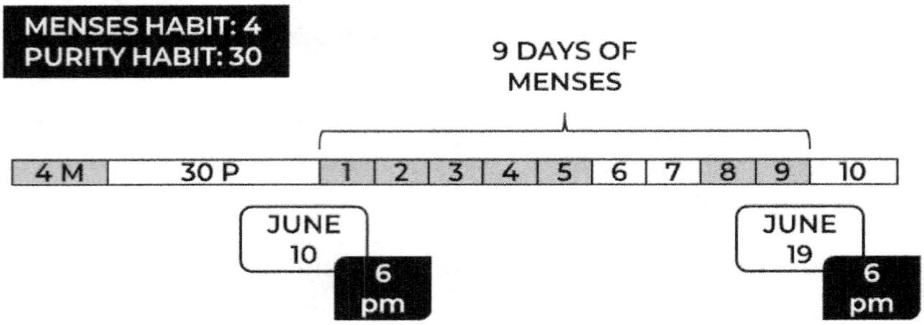

In Diagram 6.3, the bleeding returns on Day 8. It is ruled as menstruation because she is still within the possible days. Thus, she stops praying again. Days 6 and 7 are ruled as menses in retrospect, and the prayers and fasts performed on those days are invalid.

She takes another *ghusl* when the bleeding stops on Day 9. Her habit changes from 4 days to 9 days – providing that a purity span of 15 days (360 hours) follows the bleeding.

AFTER 10 DAYS:

Once the possible ten days (240 hours) have elapsed, the rulings no longer apply. If she is still bleeding, she must take a *ghusl* and begin praying. Whenever the menstrual maximum of 240 hours is reached, the bleeding thereafter is abnormal bleeding and not menstruation.

She will also return to her menses and purity habits to determine which days are ruled as menstruation, and she makes up the missed prayers beyond her menses habit.

⚠ She cannot assume that all ten days are menstruation and the next fifteen days are purity – unless those are her established habits from a previous month.

Diagram 6.4 - Blood Exceeding the Maximum

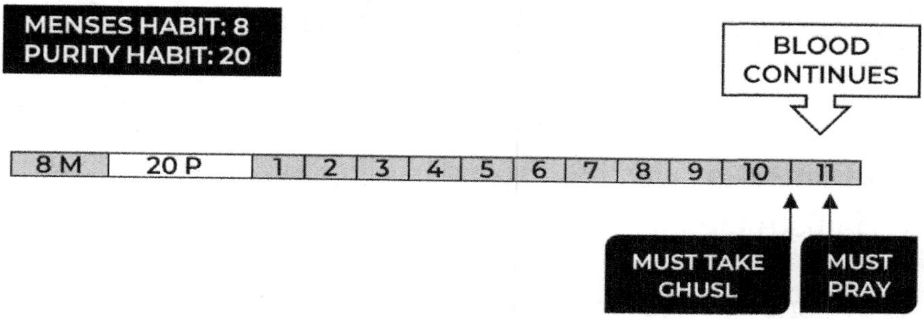

In Diagram 6.4, according to the rulings in the moment, she assumes the bleeding on Days 1 to 10 is menstruation, even though it exceeds her habit of 8 days. She does not know the future and there is no way to tell if the bleeding will stop on Day 10 or exceed the maximum.

However, once she reaches the menstrual maximum of 240 hours, she takes a *ghusl* even if she is still bleeding. The possible days of menses are over. Menstruation can be no more.

She resumes praying on Day 11. See Section 13 for related rulings.

In retrospect, because the bleeding exceeded the menstrual maximum of 240 hours, she returns to her menses and purity habits.

Thus, only Days 1 to 8 are ruled as menstruation. She makes up the missed prayers beyond her 8-day habit, which are Days 9 and 10. She must also make up any *Ramaḍān* fasts that she missed during the 10 days.

These rulings are summarized in the Possible Days of Menses Protocol.

Possible Days Of Menses Protocol

- From the onset of bleeding in a woman's expected time of menses, she has 10 possible days (240 hours) to menstruate.
- Whenever she sees blood during the possible days of menses, she acts like a menstruating woman.
- Even if the bleeding exceeds her menses habit, she continues to act like a menstruating woman.
- If the blood returns within the 10 days after having stopped, it takes the ruling of menses.
- The gaps of purity during the 10 possible days of menses are considered menstruation in retrospect.
- A *ghusl* is obligatory when menstrual bleeding either stops within the 10 possible days or the menstrual maximum of 10 complete days (240 hours) is reached.
- If the entire span of bleeding does not exceed the menstrual maximum of 240 hours, then what she sees becomes her new habit, as long as a purity span of at least 15 complete days free of blood follows it.
- She cannot consider any bleeding beyond 10 complete days (240 hours) to be menstruation. Once the menstrual maximum of 10 complete days (240 hours) is reached, menstruation can be no more.

MENSTRUAL BEGINNER:

A menstrual beginner is a girl who menstruates for the first time in her life. Islamically, she reaches puberty with her first menstruation.

This means that she is treated like a woman and not a child. Thus, she is personally responsible for praying all five obligatory prayers, fasting *Ramaḍān*, and wearing the head covering (*ḥijāb*).

After her bleeding starts, if the entire span of blood does not exceed the menstrual maximum of 240 hours and a purity span of 15 complete days (360 hours) free of blood follows it, then it becomes her menses habit. Consequently, she is no longer a menstrual beginner, but rather, she is a woman with a habit.

However, if the bleeding exceeds the menstrual maximum of 240 hours, she is given a habit of 10 complete days (240 hours) for menstruation and 20 complete days for purity. She will use these habits until her bleeding normalizes. Out of necessity, she is given a habit, and she is no longer a beginner.

If a girl reaches the age of 15 lunar years (approximately 14 solar years and six months) and she has still not experienced menstruation, she reaches puberty by age. This means that she is treated as if she physically went through puberty and is now personally responsible for her prayers, fasts, and covering.

A woman with a habit cannot given herself a menstruation habit of 10 days and a purity habit of 20 days when she experiences abnormal bleeding. This is only the case for the menstrual beginner whose bleeding exceeds 10 days.

7. The Kursuf

The *kursuf.* is a piece of cotton cloth placed **at the vaginal opening**. It is used to determine the color of discharge when it exits the vagina. It is *sunna* to wear towards the end of menses.

Once a woman removes the *kursuf,* whatever color is immediately seen will determine the legal ruling. Any change in color afterwards is of no legal consequence.

If the discharge **exits yellow** on the *kursuf* and dries white, then the discharge is considered yellow. This means that it is blood.

⇒ During the possible days of menses, it is menses.

⇒ During the days of purity, it is abnormal bleeding.

If the discharge **exits white or clear** on the *kursuf* and dries yellow, then the discharge is considered white or clear.

⇒ During the possible days of menses, it indicates that menstrual bleeding has stopped.

⇒ During the days of purity, it takes the ruling of normal vaginal discharge. See page 49.

Lighter colored discharges like yellow or turbid – in addition to normal vaginal discharge like white or clear – may change color after they exit the vagina.

Thus, the only way to ascertain the real color of these discharges is to wear a *kursuf* and to judge the discharge while it is still fresh. If the *kursuf* is worn correctly, there is hardly any chance that air will reach it and alter its color.

⚠ Pads and panty liners do not work like a *kursuf*. They are placed further away from the vaginal opening and cannot be used to determine the original color of lighter discharges.

HOW TO WEAR A KURSUF:

1. Sit on the toilet or squat.
2. Rinse the labia (lips) with water.
3. Dry the area.
4. Fold a tissue or a piece of cotton cloth into a small rectangle that is around 2 inches wide by 3 inches long.
5. Hold the folded tissue vertically. Lay the tissue on top of the labia minora (inner lips).
6. Stand up. The lips will fold over the *kursuf*, and it will not shift around or fall out while walking.

Some women feel more comfortable with using a smaller sized *kursuf*, a piece of cotton t-shirt cut to size, or a makeup remover cotton pad. Each woman should do what works for her own body.

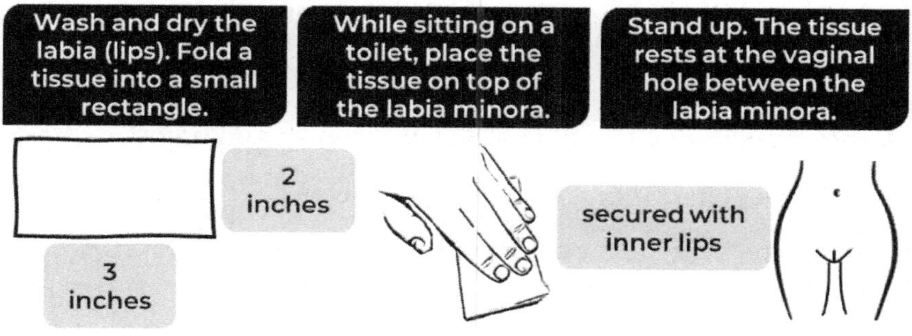

Wash and dry the labia (lips). Fold a tissue into a small rectangle.
While sitting on a toilet, place the tissue on top of the labia minora.
Stand up. The tissue rests at the vaginal hole between the labia minora.
2 inches
3 inches
secured with inner lips

8. Knowing Your Body

The Prophet ﷺ said, "Indeed, your body has a right over you."

(*Bukhārī*, 5199)

Towards the end of menstruation, it may take a longer time for the bleeding to descend to the vaginal opening. This can pose problems for a woman who sees that her panty liner is clean and takes a *ghusl*, but the bleeding later returns.

A similar issue may occur when women resort to wiping and see nothing on the toilet paper used. Some may find themselves taking a *ghusl* more than once because they assume that their menstruation has finished when in reality it has not.

Using a *kursuf* can catch scant discharge and help a woman determine if her bleeding has truly ended. When the bleeding begins to lessen to the extent that it may soon finish, a woman starts to wear the *kursuf*. It will help her to know when her bleeding officially stops.

The exact day that she chooses to use a *kursuf* to check will differ from woman to woman. As such, it is important that each woman become familiar with how her body operates. The following are practical suggestions.

As her bleeding begins to lessen, a woman should note:

- ✧ The change in colors normally seen.
- ✧ The heaviness of flow experienced.
- ✧ The number of days menses usually lasts.

Change In Colors: Some women see a spectrum of colors during their days of menstruation. The bleeding could start off with dark colors and then gradually move to lighter colors as the days pass. Perhaps the colors change from red to brown to dark yellow to light yellow and lastly to white. In this situation, it is advisable to begin wearing the *kursuf* when the light yellow is close to finishing.

Change In Flow: If she is someone who sees the same color, but her strength of flow differs from heavy to light, then she will start wearing the *kursuf* when her bleeding begins to spot. For instance, the bleeding progresses from a full flow to a light flow, and it tapers off with dots of blood. The *kursuf* is worn when spotting starts.

Change In Days: If she is someone who usually has 8 days of bleeding, then she starts to wear the *kursuf* around Day 7 when the bleeding is close to finishing.

The point is that most women have some type of recognized pattern, and each woman must discover her pattern by paying attention to her body.

How long to wear the *kursuf*: The length of time depends on each woman's body. Based on surveying many women, wearing the *kursuf* from anywhere between 30 to 90 minutes before checking is best.

The intention is to use the *kursuf* to determine whether the colored discharge has ceased; consequently, a woman should wear it for as long as she needs to achieve this goal.

It may also help to walk around to help the discharge move down towards the vaginal opening. Married woman can insert the *kursuf* inside the vagina to check. This can help catch discharge that is descending at a slower pace.

How many times to check: The *kursuf* only needs to be checked once in the prayer time and not multiple times.

Yellow or color on the *kursuf*: If the discharge exits yellow on the *kursuf*, then the discharge is ruled as yellow. This means that it is blood, and the woman is still menstruating.

White on the *kursuf*: If the discharge exits white or clear on the *kursuf* but dries into yellow, the discharge is ruled as white or clear. Within the possible days, white, clear, or no discharge marks the end of menstrual blood.

Chart 8.1 - Comparison of Discharges

DISCHARGE	QUALITIES	RULING
Menstruation or Lochia	Any color other than white or clear	*Ghusl* required upon ending & filthy
Abnormal Uterine Bleeding	Any color other than white or clear	*Wuḍū’* required & filthy
Normal Vaginal Discharge	Completely white or clear	Difference of opinion about whether it breaks *wuḍū’* and is filthy
Vaginal Infections	White, gray, or green with itch, burn, etc.	*Wuḍū’* required & filthy
Bloody Show	Pink, brown or red	*Wuḍū’* required & filthy
Arousal Fluid	Clear and sticky	*Wuḍū’* required & filthy
Orgasmic Fluid	Yellow	*Ghusl* required & filthy

OTHER VAGINAL DISCHARGES:

A woman may experience other types of vaginal discharges that are not specifically related to the *fiqh* of menstruation. The following is a breakdown of the possible vaginal discharges a woman can see.

Normal Vaginal Discharge: Looks like completely clear or white.

It is the discharge seen when a woman is not menstruating or in lochia. It is healthy for the body to excrete this discharge.

- ✧ Its color and texture change throughout the cycle. At times it can look off-white, pasty, and tacky or clear, stretchy, and gooey.
- ✧ During ovulation, copious amounts of clear discharge can look like a very pale yellow. Thus, women should not worry about seeing faint yellow discharge.

☑ There is a difference of opinion amongst scholars about whether it breaks *wuḍū'* and is filthy (*najis*).
Refer to **Question 9** in Section 17.

Section 17

Vaginal Infections: Looks like white, green, or gray discharge.

Vaginal infections can be caused by a bacteria imbalance, a yeast overgrowth, or an irritation from chemicals in female products. The discharge is accompanied with obvious signs of an infection, like:

- ✧ The discharge is clumpy like cottage cheese.
- ✧ The discharge has a fish stench.
- ✧ The vagina itches or burns.
- ✧ The vulva is inflamed or swollen.
- ✧ Sex hurts.

☑ When discharge from vaginal infections exit, it breaks *wuḍū'* and the discharge is filthy (*najis*).

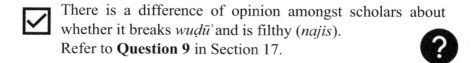

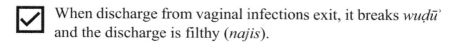

Bloody Show: Looks like pink, red, or brown discharge.

It is only experienced by pregnant women. A bloody show occurs because the cervix starts to thin and dilate in preparation for labor.

☑ When the bloody show occurs or the mucus plug is dislodged, it breaks *wuḍū'* and the discharge is filthy (*najis*).

Arousal Fluid: Looks like clear discharge. It is wet and sticky.

This fluid is produced in response to sexual stimulation, and it lubricates the vagina for the possibility of intercourse.

☑ When arousal fluid exits, it breaks *wuḍū'* and the discharge is filthy (*najis*).

Orgasmic Fluid: Looks like a thin, watery yellow.

It is experienced at the time of female ejaculation.

☑ When orgasmic fluid exits, it requires a *ghusl* and the discharge is filthy (*najis*).

These rulings are summarized in Diagram 8.1.

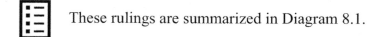

Avoid Vaginal Infections

Products like soap, bubble baths, detergents and fabric conditioners can irritate the sensitive skin around the vulva and vagina – potentially triggering an infection. Try these tips to prevent vaginal infections.

- When menstruating, change pads, panty liners, and tampons regularly.
- When showering, wash the private parts with a gentle, mild soap and warm water. There is no need to put soap directly in the vagina.
- Avoid using scented soaps and feminine products around the vagina. It can cause irritation.
- Avoid taking bubble baths. It could disrupt the vagina's natural bacteria balance.
- Avoid overly tight clothing, which can increase moisture around the private parts.
- After using the bathroom, always wipe from front to back to prevent bacteria from getting into the vagina.
- Wear 100% cotton underwear.
- Do not sit in wet clothing. Change swimsuits and wet gym clothes to dry clothing as soon as possible.

PART 4

RITUAL PURITY

Purity Defined

RITUAL STATES

- **Ritual Purity**: A state achieved after ablution (*wuḍū*ʾ), the purificatory shower (*ghusl*), or dry ablution (*tayammum*). It permits a person to pray.
- **Minor Ritual Impurity**: A state that necessitates *wuḍū*ʾ, like after sleeping, urinating, or flatulence.
- **Major Ritual Impurity**: A state that necessitates a *ghusl*, like after engaging in sexual intercourse or ejaculating (*janāba*) – as well as women in menstruation and lochia.

PHYSICAL OBJECTS

- **Pure** (*ṭāhir*): Free from all traces of physical impurity.
- **Filthy** (*najis*): Soiled with a physical impurity, like blood, urine, feces, semen, and vomit.

FIQH OF MENSTRUATION

- **Purity**: The state free of menstruation or lochia.
- **Sound Purity**: A purity span that can be taken as a habit.
- **Unsound Purity**: A purity span that cannot be used a habit.

9. The Ghusl

"Verily Allāh loves those who always turn to Him in repentance and those who purify themselves."

(*al-Baqara*, 2:222)

The **obligatory actions** of the *ghusl* are the actions that must be performed for the *ghusl* to be ruled as valid.

They are to rinse the nose, the mouth, and the entire body with water at least once. Water must reach every part of the outer body that is possible to rinse without undue hardship.

The *ghusl* is achieved with the use of water. There is no requirement to use soap, shampoo, or conditioner.

During the *ghusl* a woman must:

- ☑ Rinse the inside of the nose, the inside of the mouth, and the entire outer body with water at least once.
- ☑ Ensure that water reaches all of her hair, underneath the skin of the clitoral hood, the external orifice of the genitals, and the skin underneath the eyebrows.
- ☑ Wet the inside of the belly button and the inside of any hole that is not sealed, like earring holes.

In the *Ḥanafī madhhab*, making the intention to perform the *ghusl* is not obligatory, but rather it is a *sunna* action.

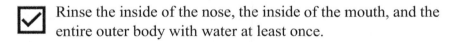

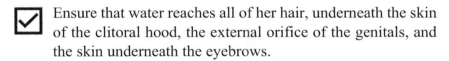

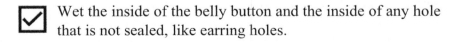

STEP-BY-STEP GHUSL WITH SUNNA ACTS:

1. Make an intention in the heart to perform the *ghusl* for the sake of Allāh Most High, while saying '*bismi Llahir Raḥmānir Raḥīm*' with the tongue before revealing one's nakedness (*'awra*).

   This should be done while also washing the hands up to the wrists.

2. Wash away any filth (*najāsa*) on any part of the body.

3. Wash both the front and the back private parts, even if they are free from filth (*najāsa*).

4. Perform a complete *wuḍū'* with the *sunna* actions like what is done for the prayer.

5. Pour water over the body three times, making sure that the entire body is rinsed each time. This is easily achieved under a shower head.

   It is related that one first begins with the head, then continues with the right shoulder, then the left shoulder, and then rinses the remainder of the body. Repeat three times.

It is *sunna* to use the hand to help the water flow along the limbs (*dalk*) during the first washing, and thereafter it is recommended. The body parts should be washed successively.

It is from proper manners (*adab*) that one does not face the *qibla*, talk, or say *dhikr* aloud while naked.

SUNNA PURIFICATION HABITS:

Based on the habits learned from the *sunna*, it is best to take a *ghusl*, clip one's nails, and remove armpit and pubic hair once a week, with preference given to Friday.

If this is not possible, then these actions are performed every 15 days. It is sinful to leave them for more than 40 days.

Any method used for hair removal is permissible, such as shaving, waxing, or creams, providing that it does not cause harm to the body.

The *sunna* for removing hair under the arms is achieved by plucking, although shaving is acceptable too.

It is not permitted to expose one's nakedness (*ʿawra*) to others while removing pubic hair, even if it be with another women. The *ʿawra* of a woman in the company of another woman is from her navel to her knee.

Women who are at work and cannot leave to take a *ghusl* should refer to the answer in **Question 11** in Section 17.

Section 17

10. The Ghusl Time

The *ghusl* time is a technical term that refers to the amount of time it takes to prepare for the *ghusl*, complete the obligatory acts of the *ghusl*, and get ready for the prayer. Scholars estimate the *ghusl* time to be no longer than 15 minutes in today's times.

ADDING THE GHUSL TIME TO THE HABIT:

✔ When bleeding ends **before** the menstrual maximum of 240 hours, the *ghusl* time is **added** to the menses habit. View a sample record in Section 5 with Chart 5.5.

✖ When bleeding ends **at** the menstrual maximum of 240 hours, the *ghusl* time is **not** added to the menses habit.

DELAYING THE GHUSL:

✔ When a woman's menstruation stops **before** her habit, there is a strong possibility that the bleeding may return. Therefore, it is obligatory for her to delay taking her *ghusl* until closer to the end of the prayer time.

For example, her menses habit is 9 days and her bleeding stops on Day 5. She should delay taking her *ghusl* just in case the bleeding returns. If she does not see blood again in the prayer time, she takes a *ghusl* and prays.

✔ If her menstruation stops **at or after** her habit, then delaying the *ghusl* is recommended and not required.

If her menstruation stops **at** the maximum, then there is no need to delay the *ghusl*. The possible days are over.

For the *'Aṣr* prayer time, she delays the *ghusl* until closer to the end of the preferred prayer time, which is before the prohibitively disliked time enters.

ENGAGING IN SEXUAL INTERCOURSE:

When bleeding ends **before** the habit, a woman is obliged to take a *ghusl*, but she cannot engage in sexual intercourse until her habit elapses.

In Diagram 10.1, her menses habit is 9 full days. When her bleeding stops on Day 5, she takes a *ghusl* and begins praying. She cannot engage in sexual intercourse until her 9-day habit elapses on Day 10.

Diagram 10.1 - Blood Stops Before the Habit

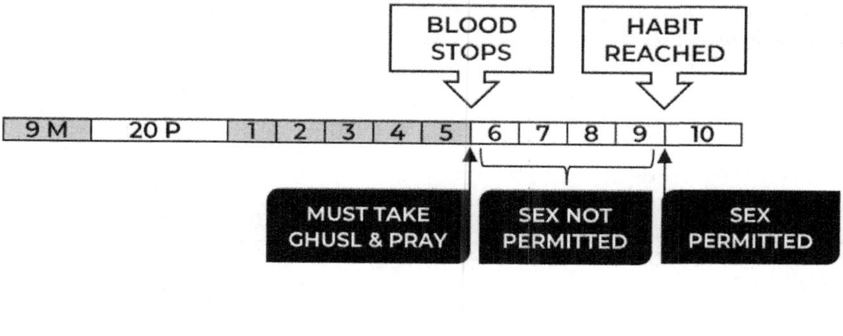

When bleeding ends **at or after** the habit, a woman is obliged to take a *ghusl*, and sexual intercourse is permissible any time afterwards.

In Diagram 10.2, her menses habit is 4 days. If her bleeding stops on Day 4 or thereafter, she takes a *ghusl* and sexual intercourse is permitted.

Diagram 10.2 - Blood Stops After the Habit

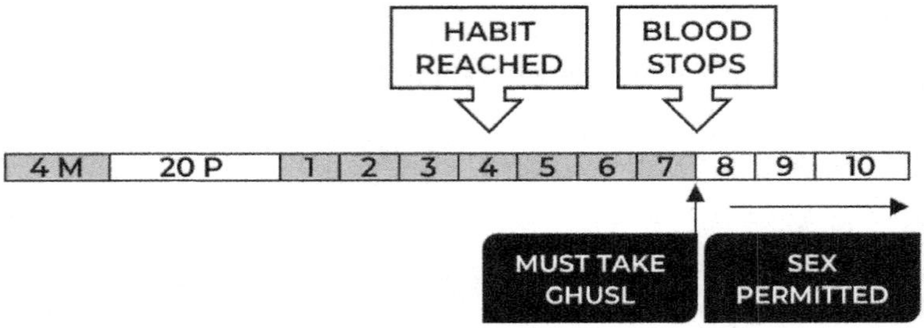

When bleeding ends **at** the maximum of 240 hours, a woman is obliged to take a *ghusl* and sex is permitted.

Chart 10.3 - Summary of Rulings

Blood Ends	Before Habit	At / After Habit	At Maximum
Ghusl Time	Included in the habit.	Included in the habit.	Not included in habit.
Delaying the Ghusl	Required to wait until closer to the end of the prayer time.	Recommended to wait until closer to the end of the prayer time.	Does not apply because the possible days are over.
Marital Relations	Impermissible until the habit is complete.	Impermissible until after the *ghusl*.	Permissible

11. Sound Purity Simplified

The Prophet ﷺ said, "Purity is half of faith."

(*Muslim*, 223)

The purity span (*ṭuhr*) generally refers to a duration that is not considered menstruation or lochia. Thus, during her purity span, a woman can pray, fast, read the Qur'ān, touch the Qur'ān, have sexual intercourse, and the like.

There is a need for a woman to experience a purity span after her menstrual bleeding ends. Otherwise, she cannot consider the next show of blood to be menstruation. The same applies to the bleeding that follows lochia.

- **Between a menstruation and a menstruation**: A minimal duration of 15 complete days (360 hours) free of blood must occur for the second bleeding to be ruled as menstruation.

- **Between a lochia and a menstruation**: A minimal duration of 15 complete days (360 hours) free of blood must occur for the second bleeding to be ruled as menstruation.

As for the maximum duration of purity, there is none. A purity span can technically last a lifetime.

THE SOUND PURITY:

The sound purity (*aṭ-ṭuhr aṣ-ṣaḥīḥ*) is the only purity that can be taken as a habit. It has three conditions, and all three conditions must be met without exception.

- It lasts for a duration of **at least** 15 complete days (360 hours) or more.
- It is free from blood during this **entire** span. This includes the colors brown and fresh yellow.
- It occurs between two **sound** bloods. For example, it occurs between two menses, or a lochia and a menses.

A woman's purity habit is established with the most recent purity that she sees, providing that it fulfills all the conditions of a sound purity. She only needs to see it occur once for the habit to be established, and she is obliged to record it.

⚠ If any of these conditions are not met, the purity is unsound, and it cannot be taken as a habit. She may need to revise her situation with a teacher too.

Diagram 11.1 - Establishing A Purity Habit

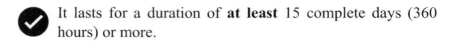

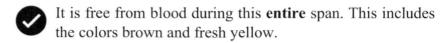

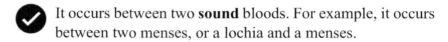

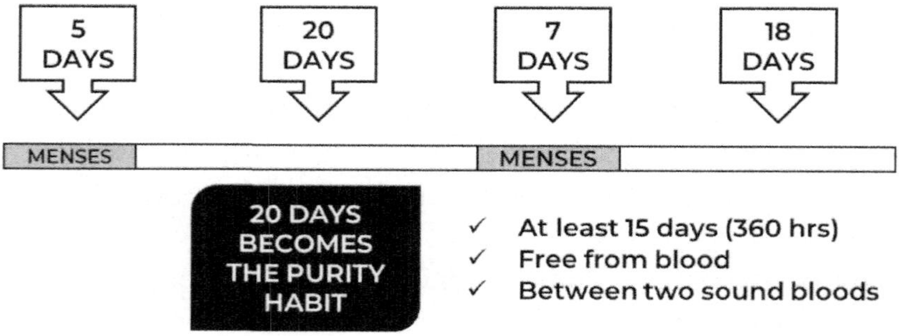

In Diagram 11.1, her menstruation of 5 days is followed by 20 days free of blood, and then 7 days of menstruation. The purity span of 20 days becomes her habit because it meets all the conditions of a sound purity.

12. Abnormal Bleeding

Abnormal uterine bleeding (*istiḥāḍa*) is any colored vaginal discharge that is not ruled as menses or lochia. It is unsound blood, and it can never be taken as a habit.

- It can be any color, whether it be red, brown, or fresh yellow.
- It can be spotting or a constant flow.
- It can be seen at any time within the month.

A woman must continue to perform her obligatory worship of praying and fasting *Ramaḍān*, even though she is seeing blood. She is also permitted to engage in sexual intercourse no matter how heavy the flow.

Chart 12.1 - Comparison Between Different Types of Blood

ACTION	MENSES & LOCHIA	ABNORMAL BLEEDING
Obligatory Prayers	Unlawful	Obligatory with *wuḍū'*
Obligatory Fasts	Unlawful	Obligatory
***Sunna / Nafl* Prayers**	Unlawful	Permissible with *wuḍū'*
***Sunna / Nafl* Fasts**	Unlawful	Permissible
Touching the Qur'ān	Unlawful	Permissible with *wuḍū'*
Reciting the Qur'ān	Unlawful	Permissible
Entering the Mosque	Unlawful	Permissible
Making *Ṭawāf*	Unlawful	Permissible with *wuḍū'*
Marital Relations	Unlawful	Permissible

IDENTIFYING ABNORMAL BLEEDING:

Fluctuations within the stipulated ranges of menstruation and lochia are normal and expected.

However, if the bleeding does not abide by the definitions and conditions of menstruation or lochia, then it will be ruled as abnormal bleeding.

There are different ways that this can happen. At a basic level, a woman knows that she has an abnormal bleeding problem when:

- Her bleeding is less than the menstrual minimum of three days (72 hours).
- Her bleeding exceeds the menstrual maximum of 10 days (240 hours) or the lochia maximum of 40 days (960 hours).
- Her bleeding is not followed by a purity of at least 15 days (360 hours). See **Question 12** in Section 17.
- She sees colored discharge during her purity span.

Section 17

A woman in this situation should contact a teacher and ask for help.

Refer to **Questions 14 and 15** in Section 17 for more information about abnormal bleeding.

Section 17

Recommended Readings from the Appendix:

- Istihada: What Is It With Examples
- IUD & Istihada

13. Praying While Bleeding

"Strive for (seeking the pleasure of) Allāh, a striving that is owed to Him. He has chosen you and did not impose any hardship on you in the religion."

(al-Ḥajj, 22:78)

For a woman experiencing abnormal bleeding, certain rulings may be relaxed due to her situation. Constant abnormal bleeding (*istiḥāḍa*) can be uncomfortable and challenging.

However, Allāh Most High provides a way for her to practice her religion and continue to pray with the Excused Person's Rulings despite her circumstance.

Every woman's abnormal bleeding situation will be unique. Some women may see occasional spotting, while others may experience a constant flow of blood.

Therefore, the rulings related to how a woman will pray are dependent upon two factors:

- Whether the blood **continues** to exit her vagina while she is making *wuḍū'* or praying the obligatory prayer.

- Whether she possesses the **ability to stop** the blood flow for this duration.

SPOTTING:

If she is spotting, there may not be a need for her to resort to the Excused Person's Rulings. She can wash her private parts, make *wuḍūʾ*, and pray her obligatory prayer.

If **no** bleeding exits her vagina while doing so, then what she has done is sufficient for her prayer to count. She is treated as a normal person with regards to *wuḍūʾ* and her prayers.

CONSTANT FLOW:

A constant flow of blood means that a woman does **not** have the ability to make *wuḍūʾ* and pray the obligatory prayer of the current time without vaginal blood exiting. The rulings will differ for a virgin and a non-virgin.

⇒ Women who are virgins will always use the Excused Person's Rulings, providing that they fulfill the conditions for establishing the excuse.

⇒ Women who are non-virgins must first try to block the blood flow from exiting the vagina, providing that it is not harmful for her and she is not fasting. Blocking can be done with any material, like a tampon or a tissue.

If she can make *wuḍūʾ* and pray the obligatory prayer without bleeding exiting the vagina, then this is sufficient for her prayer to count, and she is treated as a normal person with regards to *wuḍūʾ* and her prayers.

If despite taking the means to block, a woman's flow is very heavy such that the bleeding cannot be stopped from exiting during her entire *wuḍūʾ* and the obligatory prayer, then she will resort to the Excused Person's Rulings.

THE EXCUSED PERSON:

With the Excused Person's Rulings, a woman with abnormal bleeding can make *wuḍū'*, and even if the bleeding continues to flow from her vagina, her *wuḍū'* remains valid.

She can perform regular acts of worship – such as praying, making *ṭawāf,* and touching the Qur'ān – without being obliged to renew her *wuḍū'* within the same prayer time.

As previously mentioned, the Excused Person's Rulings do not necessarily apply to every woman who is experiencing abnormal bleeding. The matter returns to if she can establish the excuse and maintain the excuse based on the conditions stated by scholars. These conditions are briefly outlined in Diagram 13.1, and their details can be found in the recommended readings.

Diagram 13.1 - Conditions for the Excused Person

ESTABLISH EXCUSED STATUS	•Vaginal bleeding is constant, such that she cannot make *wuḍū'* and pray the obligatory (*farḍ*) prayer without the excuse occurring. This inability to keep *wuḍū'* lasts for an entire prescribed (*farḍ*) prayer time.
MAINTAIN EXCUSED STATUS	•The vaginal bleeding occurs at least once in every subsequent prayer time.
LOSE EXCUSED STATUS	•The vaginal bleeding does not occur for an entire prescribed prayer time.

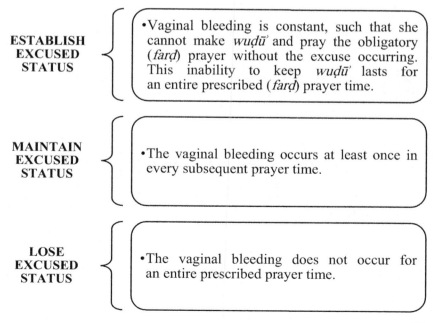

PRAYING WITH BLOOD:

If a woman prays with a spot of blood on her clothes or body that is less than the size of a *dirham* (about five centimeters in diameter), it is slightly disliked (*makrūh tanzīhān*).

Thus, it is recommended to remove the blood before praying – although the prayer is valid if it is not removed.

If a woman prays with more than this amount on her clothes or body, and she has the means to remove it, the prayer is not valid.

REMOVING BLOOD:

To purify clothes soiled with blood, the soiled area must be washed with water until the body of the blood is removed. If this is achieved through one washing under running water, it is sufficient.

- ✧ Using soap is not a condition.
- ✧ Stains that remain after the washing are excused.

It is best to wash the soiled area with water before putting the garment in the washing machine.

Recommended Readings from the Appendix:

- The Excused Person's Rulings: A Complete Breakdown
- How to Pray With Istihada

Hamna's Story

Ḥamna bint Jaḥsh ※ experienced a situation of excessive abnormal bleeding. 'Imrān ibn Ṭalḥa ※ relates that his mother, Ḥamna ※, said:

> "I had blood flow that was plentiful and severe. So, I went to the Prophet ※ to ask and inform him about it. I found him ※ in the house of my sister, Zaynab bint Jaḥsh ※. I said, 'O Messenger of Allāh! I suffer from excessive and severe blood flow. So, what do you command me to do concerning it? It is preventing me from praying and fasting.' He ※ said: 'Insert a *kursuf* for it will block the blood flow.' Ḥamna ※ responded, 'It is more than that.' He ※ said, 'Tighten it to your body like a belt.' Ḥamna ※ responded, 'It is more than that.' He ※ said, 'Use a cloth.' Ḥamna ※ responded, 'It is more than that. Indeed, I am bleeding heavily.'"

(Tirmidhī, 128; Aḥmad, 27475; ibn Mājah, 627)

Ḥamna's ※ bleeding was copious, to the extent that she thought it should prevent her from praying and fasting. In *Tirmidhī*'s version, the story continues with the Prophet ※ affirming that her abnormal bleeding is not menstruation, but it is a "…kick from the devil."

Scholars explain that what is meant by a kick is that the devil will come to women during this time and try to confuse them. He will make them doubt their habit and convince them that the blood is menstruation so that they leave their worship. Therefore, women with abnormal bleeding must be mindful of the devil's plotting and take care to not fall prey to his tricks.

PART 5

MATERNITY MATTERS

A Mother's Reward

رَبَّنَا هَبْ لَنَا مِنْ أَزْوَاجِنَا وَذُرِّيَّاتِنَا قُرَّةَ أَعْيُنٍ وَاجْعَلْنَا لِلْمُتَّقِينَ إِمَامًا

Rabbanā hab lanā min azwājinā wa dhurriyyātinā qurrata ʾaʿyun wajʿalnā lil muttaqīna imāmā

"Our Lord! Bless us with pious spouses and offspring who will be the joy of our hearts and make us models for the righteous."

(*al-Furqān,* 25:74)

The act of carrying a child in the womb, as well as overcoming the challenges that come with pregnancy, is worship. Consequently, a pregnant woman must not miss out on this golden opportunity to draw nearer to her Lord.

She should be dutiful in her prayers, increase in her recitation of the Qurʾān, and make abundant *dhikr* of Allāh Most High.

She should fuel her body with lawful food and avoid anything that is unlawful or dubious.

She must also frequently pray to Allāh to aid her in her struggles and ask Him for help with raising her child.

The constant sacrifices that a mother makes are only known to Allāh Most High. Yet, she will be rewarded for her actions on the Day of Judgement if she practices a beautiful patience for His sake.

14. Pregnancy

Any blood or colored vaginal discharge seen during pregnancy is considered abnormal bleeding (*istiḥāḍa*).

However, seeing blood during pregnancy is not normal. A pregnant woman should notify her doctor of the bleeding out of safety for herself and her child. She should also keep a record of any blood that she experiences due to the possibility of miscarrying, which may change the rulings in retrospect for her situation.

As for her worship, even if she is experiencing abnormal bleeding, she must continue to pray until she gives birth. During labor, any blood or fluid that exits **before** childbirth is considered filthy (*najis*), and it does not lift the obligation to pray.

Even if a woman is experiencing contractions, she must pray until actual childbirth. The advice from many mothers is to pray as soon as the prayer time comes in, if this is possible. The sooner a woman prays, the less worry it is for her.

When contractions become more intense, it may not be easy or possible to bow as usual or prostrate on the floor. In this circumstance, a woman may need to resort to the sick person's rulings for her prayer. These rulings permit a person to pray sitting up or lying down with head movements. More information can be found in the recommended readings.

Recommended Readings from the Appendix:

- Praying While Sitting During Pregnancy
- Five Must-Know Rulings For Praying During Labor
- The Sick Person's Prayer With Pictures

15. Lochia Simplified

"My Lord! Be merciful to them as they raised me when I was young."

(*al-Isrā', 17:24*)

Lochia (*nifās*) is blood that originates from the uterus and comes out of the vagina after childbirth. The blood from the incision of a cesarean section is not lochia; rather, only the vaginal bleeding that exits after the operation is lochia.

Lochia has no minimum and its maximum is 40 complete days (960 hours).

Diagram 15.1 - When Possible Days Begin

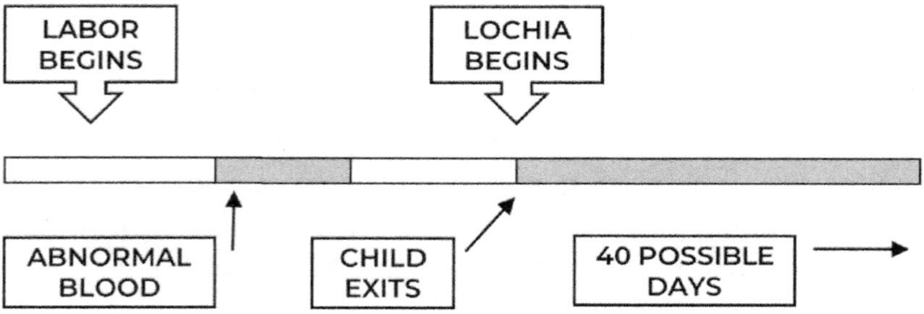

POSSIBLE DAYS OF LOCHIA:

After the baby exits, a woman has 40 potential days to experience lochia, which is known as the possible days of lochia. There are two rulings related to the possible days:

1 **Whenever blood is seen within the possible days of lochia, it is always considered lochia.**

⇒ This includes any color of blood, like brown and turbid.

⇒ It also includes bleeding that is spotting, a light flow, or blood that stops and returns within the possible days.

⇒ A woman will not pray, fast, or engage in any of the prohibited acts while seeing blood in her possible days.

2 **Whenever blood stops within the possible days, it is ruled as lochia, and she is obliged to take a *ghusl* and pray.**

⇒ The sign that the bleeding has stopped is that she sees clear, white, or no discharge – and she is certain that the blood will not return.

⇒ She must take a *ghusl* before praying.

⇒ She is not required to make up any prayers missed during lochia, but she must make up her *Ramaḍān* fasts.

⇒ If blood returns within the possible days, it is lochia and she takes another *ghusl* when the blood stops. The worship performed in-between the two shows of blood is invalid and these days become lochia in retrospect.

✓ If the entire span of bleeding does not exceed the lochia maximum of 960 hours, then it becomes her new lochia habit – providing that a purity span of 15 complete days (360 hours) free of blood follows it and it ends outside the 40 days.

In Diagram 15.2, a woman with a 25-day lochia habit bleeds for 30 days after childbirth, and then she sees 20 days of purity before bleeding starts again. The purity span ends outside the 40 possible days of lochia. Her habit changes from 25 days to 30 days.

Diagram 15.2 - Purity Span After Lochia

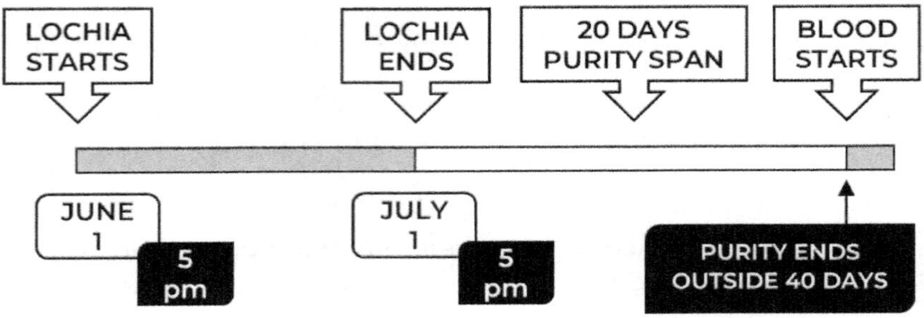

AFTER 40 DAYS:

Once the possible 40 days (960 hours) have elapsed, the rulings no longer apply.

If she is still bleeding, she must take a *ghusl* and begin praying. Whenever the lochia maximum is reached, the bleeding thereafter is abnormal bleeding and not lochia.

She will also return to her lochia and purity habits to determine which days are ruled as lochia, and she makes up the missed prayers beyond her lochia habit.

⚠ She cannot assume that all 40 days are lochia – unless this is her first baby or it was her established lochia habit from a previous birth or miscarriage.

In Diagram 15.3, a woman bleeds for 41 days after giving birth. Once the lochia maximum (960 hours) is reached, she takes a *ghusl* and starts praying on Day 41.

Because she has previously given birth, she returns to her lochia habit, which is 38 days. In retrospect, Days 39 and 40 are ruled as abnormal bleeding and not lochia. She must make up the prayers missed on these days. She must also make up any *Ramaḍān* fasts that she missed during the 40 days.

Diagram 15.3 - Lochia Bleeding Exceeds the Maximum

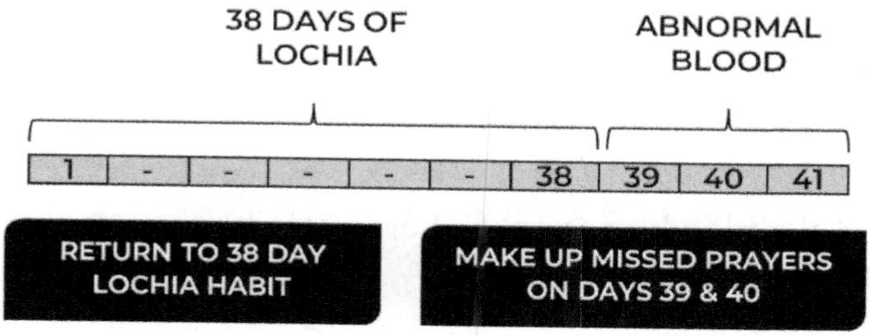

These rulings are summarized in the Possible Days of Lochia Protocol.

LOCHIA BEGINNER:

A lochia beginner is a woman who is giving birth for the first time in her life.

After she gives birth, if the entire span of bleeding does not exceed the lochia maximum of 40 days (960 hours) and a purity span of 15 complete days (360 hours) free of blood follows it, then it becomes her lochia habit. She is no longer a beginner.

However, if the bleeding exceeds the lochia maximum of 960 hours, she is given a habit of 40 complete days (960 hours). If needed, she will use this lochia habit for future births or miscarriages. She is no longer a beginner.

Possible Days Of Lochia Protocol

- After childbirth, a woman has 40 possible days (960 hours) to experience lochia.
- Whenever she sees blood during the possible days of lochia, she acts like a menstruating woman.
- Even if the bleeding exceeds her lochia habit, she continues to abide by the prohibitions.
- If the blood returns within the 40 days after having stopped, it takes the ruling of lochia.
- The gaps of purity during the 40 possible days of lochia are considered lochia in retrospect.
- A *ghusl* is obligatory when bleeding either stops within the 40 possible days or the lochia maximum of 40 complete days (960 hours) is reached.
- If the entire span of bleeding does not exceed the maximum of 960 hours, then what she sees becomes her new habit, as long as a purity span of at least 15 complete days free of blood follows it and it ends outside the 40 days.
- She cannot consider any bleeding beyond 40 complete days (960 hours) to be lochia. Once the maximum of 40 complete days (960 hours) is reached, lochia can be no more.

THE GHUSL:

The *ghusl* taken when lochia ends is the same *ghusl* described in Section 9. The rulings related to the *ghusl* time in Section 10 apply when lochia bleeding ends. Replace the word menses with lochia (and 240 hours with 960 hours) to know the ruling.

TWINS:

With twins and triplets, lochia begins with the exiting of most of the first baby according to Imām Abū Ḥanīfa. A span of at least six months must separate between two lochia. If the span is less than six months, the babies are considered twins and share the same days of lochia.

MENSTRUATION AFTER LOCHIA:

After a woman's lochia ends, she must see a purity span of at least 15 complete days (360 hours) before any bleeding can be considered menstruation.

For many women, breastfeeding causes their hormones to fluctuate, and some may not see menstrual bleeding for an entire year after giving birth. Others experience abnormal bleeding and spotting.

If a woman is experiencing abnormal bleeding, her problem is resolved by using her menses and purity habits that she had from before her pregnancy.

MISCARRIAGES:

Section 17

As for the bleeding seen due to a miscarriage, the ruling is dependent upon what a woman miscarries. Refer to **Question 13** in Section 17.

PART 6

CONCLUDING TOPICS

Allah Loves

DOERS OF GOOD	الْمُحْسِنِيْنَ
CONSTANT REPENTERS	التَّوَّابِيْنَ
THE GOD FEARING	الْمُتَّقِيْنَ
THE PATIENT	الصَّابِرِيْنَ
THOSE RELYING ON HIM	الْمُتَوَكِّلِيْنَ
THE JUST	الْمُقْسِطِيْنَ

16. Menopause

Menopause is the end of menstruation. It is a natural biological process that all women are destined to experience. Once a woman reaches menopause, she will no longer be able to have children.

The age of menopause is 55 lunar years (approximately 53 solar years and 4 months). If a woman reaches the age of menopause and her menstrual cycles have stopped, she is deemed to be a menopausal woman.

COLORED DISCHARGE AFTER MENOPAUSE:

If she continues to see colored vaginal discharge after 55 lunar years, as a general principle, it is **not** menstruation. Instead, the discharge is ruled as abnormal bleeding (*istiḥāḍa*).

THE EXCEPTION:

However, an exception to this principle is if the discharge is black, red, or like her pre-menopausal period.

- Black means a very dark red.
- Red refers to the usual color of blood.
- Her pre-menopausal period means the colors that she saw during her menstruation before she reached menopause. For example, maybe she only menstruated with the color brown.

In such a case, the bleeding could be ruled as menstruation if it meets the menstrual minimum and the other conditions for menstruation that were previously stated in Section 5.

In Diagram 16.1, a woman who has reached menopause at 55 lunar years sees two months free of blood and then she bleeds for four days.

The blood is red, and it reaches the menstrual minimum of three days (72 hours). It was also preceded by a purity span of at least 15 days (360 hours).

Therefore, the blood is ruled as menstruation, even though she is 55 lunar years old.

Diagram 16.1 - Red Blood After 55 Lunar Years

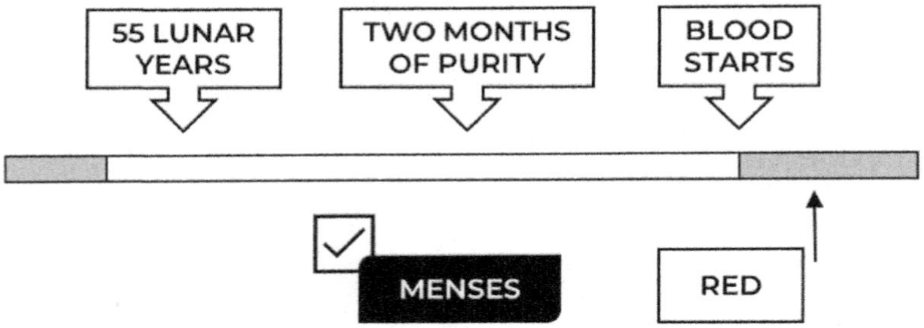

A woman will undergo many physical changes as she continues to age, but her aging should not hold her back from doing what it takes to please Allāh Most High. Age is just a number; what matters the most is how much she blossomed in her life for Allah Most High.

17. Popular Questions

"My Lord! Increase me in knowledge!"

(*Ṭāhā, 20:114*)

Q1: What if I never recorded my bleeding?

Start now. If you are experiencing abnormal bleeding, then make a reasoned judgement about when you last saw a sound blood and contact a teacher. If this is not possible, you can try taking hormonal medication to regulate your bleeding and establish a habit.

Q2: Why do I make up the fasts missed for *Ramaḍān* and not my obligatory prayers?

This is what the Prophet ﷺ commanded the female Companions ﵂ to do.

Scholars state that the wisdom in making up the missed fasts and not the missed prayers is based upon *Ramaḍān* only occurring once a year. Making up approximately ten fasts (or less) a year is not difficult – as opposed to making up the missed prayers every month for an entire year.

Recommended Readings from the Appendix:
- Menstruation Rulings Related to Ramadan
- Worship In Ramadan for a Menstruating Woman
- Taking Medication To Delay Menstruation in Ramadan

Q3: Can I touch my phone when a Qurʾān app is open?

There is a difference of opinion amongst contemporary scholars.

- The more precautionary opinion is that when the app is open and verses appear on the screen, it is not permissible to hold the device or touch its screen without ritual purity – unless it is done with a pen or barrier.

- Another opinion is that when the app is open and verses are on the screen, it is permissible to hold the device, but it is not permissible to touch the screen without ritual purity.

According to both views, when the app is closed, the device takes the ruling of a phone or tablet, and it can be touched without ritual purity.

Q4: Can I recite the Qurʾān for *tajwīd* classes?

It is not permitted to recite the Qurʾān during menstruation or lochia, even if it is for a class. As for a Qurʾān teacher, she is permitted to dictate the verse word-by-word, taking a pause between each word. If this poses difficulty, it may help to ask a scholar about the Mālikī *madhhab*'s position. You can also read about the Mālikī *madhhab*'s position in Article 13 in the recommended readings in the Appendix.

Q5: Which *ḥajj* rites can a menstruating woman perform?

It is permissible for a menstruating woman to enter into a state of *iḥrām* for *ḥajj* and *ʿumra*. It is also permissible to take the *sunna ghusl* for *iḥrām* beforehand.

As for the *ḥajj* rites, it is permissible for a menstruating woman to perform the standing at ʿArafat (*wuqūf*), spend the night at

Muzdalifa, camp at Minā, stone the *jamarāt*, and perform the slaughtering.

She cannot perform the *ṭawāf*, pray the ritual prayer, or enter the mosque.

Recommended Readings from the Appendix:

- Umra Rites During Menstruation
- Umra Advice and Answers for Menstruating Women
- Medication to Block Menstrual Blood During Umra

Q6: Does arousal fluid break *wuḍū*?

Arousal fluid is a clear, sticky discharge that is produced in response to sexual stimulation. When arousal fluid exits, it breaks *wuḍū*ʾ and the discharge is filthy (*najis*). When orgasmic fluid exits due to ejaculation, it requires a *ghusl*. Refer to Section 8.

Q7: Is green discharge a color of blood?

Light green discharge is usually a sign of a vaginal infection, and it is not menses. It breaks *wuḍū*ʾ and is filthy (*najis*).

Q8: Is yellow discharge a color of blood?

Fresh yellow is a color of blood. Yellow that is dried on a panty liner is disregarded. Using a *kursuf* helps to know what color the discharge was when it exited the vagina. Refer to Section 7 and 8.

It is important to note that during ovulation, copious amounts of clear discharge can look like a very pale yellow. Thus, women should not worry about seeing faint yellow discharge.

Q9: Does normal vaginal discharge break *wuḍūʾ*?

Normal vaginal discharge is the discharge seen when a woman is not menstruating or in lochia. It is completely clear or white in color.

The more precautionary position is that its exiting breaks *wuḍūʾ* and it is filthy (*najis*). However, there is another followable position that normal vaginal discharge is pure and it does not break *wuḍūʾ*. According to this position, a woman would not need to renew her *wuḍūʾ* or change her panty liner before praying.

Q10: Is spotting while taking birth control considered menstruation?

Your doctor may inform you that any breakthrough bleeding seen while on birth control or other hormonal medications is not menstruation. What doctors mean is that the bleeding you are experiencing is not caused by ovulation, which is what happens with your body's natural menstrual cycle.

However, from an Islamic perspective, experiencing ovulation is not a condition for menstruation. Thus, if the bleeding falls within your expected time of menstruation, then it is ruled as menstruation, providing that the bleeding meets the menstrual minimum of three complete days (72 hours).

This ruling also applies to spotting because there is no condition for menstrual bleeding to be constant.

Q11: What if I am at work and cannot take a *ghusl*?

Firstly, you should take all means possible to leave work and take a *ghusl*. For example, perhaps you could take a half day off or check into a gym with a shower near your job during lunch break.

If this is not possible, then out of the sanctity of the prayer time, some modern-day scholars say that you can make *tayammum* with pure earth and pray within the designated time. However, when you return home, you must take a *ghusl* and makeup the prayers.

Q12: What if my bleeding starts before 15 days (360 hours) of purity is reached?

If bleeding starts before 15 days of purity is reached, a woman returns to her menses and purity habits. She cannot consider the new blood to be menstruation if it falls outside her expected time of menses. Furthermore, she cannot stop praying after 15 days are complete, unless 15 days is her purity habit.

There are other rulings related to bleeding starting earlier than expected – specifically after a 15-day purity elapses but before the purity habit is reached. Refer to the Chapter 18: Early Blood Formula in "A Muslim Woman's Guide to Menstruation Rulings."

Q13: What is the ruling for blood after a miscarriage?

There are two types of miscarriages: a miscarriage of an undeveloped embryo and a miscarriage of a developed fetus.

A developed fetus means that the fetus has developed a human feature, like a nail, a toe, or a finger, as opposed to being a blood clot or clump of flesh.

A woman keeps her pregnancy status with the miscarriage of a developed fetus. Therefore, the blood seen after the miscarriage of a developed fetus is lochia.

For an undeveloped embryo, a woman loses the status of pregnancy and she must return to her menses and purity habits. This means that the blood seen before and after the miscarriage is menstruation if it falls within the time of menses; otherwise, it is abnormal bleeding.

Q14: If I am experiencing abnormal bleeding, how do I know when my menstruation begins?

Whenever a woman experiences abnormal bleeding, she must use her menstrual and purity habits to determine which part of the bleeding is considered menstruation. This is why it is important to record your habits.

As a general rule, any colored discharge that falls within the expected time of menstruation is ruled as menstruation, providing that the definition and conditions for menstruation are met.

It is advisable to contact a teacher to help you. Depending on how complicated your situation is, various rulings may be used to help you.

Q15: Why am I experiencing abnormal bleeding?

It is best to consult a doctor about one's specific symptoms for a more precise understanding.

Some possible reasons could be:

- Stress and lifestyle changes
- Birth control / IUD
- Hormonal imbalances
- Polycystic ovary syndrome (PCOS)
- Uterine polyps or fibroids
- Endometriosis
- Reactions to medications
- Implantation bleeding from pregnancy

- Pregnancy complications
- Miscarriages, like an ectopic pregnancy
- Endometrial hyperplasia

HEALING ABNORMAL BLEEDING

To diagnose a woman with a potential cause for abnormal bleeding, a doctor will most likely do all or some of the following:

- Perform a physical exam like a pelvic ultrasound.
- Request a pap smear.
- Request a pregnancy test.
- Request a blood test.
- Request a thyroid test or hormone levels test.
- Consider investigative procedures like a hysteroscopy.

Once a reason has been identified, medications may be prescribed to help reduce or regulate the bleeding, like birth control pills.

Alternatively, many women choose to embark on their own healing journey and resolve their abnormal bleeding through natural means.

Natural healing methods can consist of:

- Altering dietary choices.
- Treating vitamin deficiencies.
- Engaging in daily exercise.
- Getting womb, pelvic, or body massages.
- Taking homeopathy remedies.
- Practicing stress reduction exercises.
- Undergoing trauma treatment.

Each woman's situation is unique, and every woman must choose the options that are best for her circumstance.

APPENDIX

رَبَّنَا تَقَبَّلْ مِنَّآ إِنَّكَ أَنتَ
ٱلسَّمِيعُ ٱلْعَلِيمُ

OUR LORD!
ACCEPT (THIS SERVICE)
FROM US. INDEED YOU ARE
THE ALL-HEARING,
THE ALL-KNOWING.

(2:127)

About the Author

All praise is due to Allah, Lord of the Worlds. May peace and blessings be upon His beloved Messenger ﷺ.

Naielah Ackbarali is the founder and CEO of Muslima Coaching. She studied various Islamic sciences with top traditional scholars in both Syria and Jordan for over 15 years. She is currently continuing her advanced Islamic studies in England.

Naielah is a trained strategic relationship coach, certified life coach, and a certified NLP Master Practitioner. Combined with her knowledge from Islamic studies, coaching experience, and personal marriage of more than 15 years, she offers faith-based marriage coaching to couples, wives, and singles.

She is an author of several books and has been featured on the Islam Channel and British Muslim TV.

Naielah has also written:

- "**A Muslim Woman's Guide To Menstruation Rulings**" an intermediate guide for women ages 17+.
- **"Blossom: A Muslim Girl's Puberty Guide"** for girls ages 9 to 14.
- "Ramadan Ready: Action Steps for Muslim Women" for women and teens.
- "Secrets of Successful Muslim Couples: Marriage Tips for a Lifetime" for spouses.
- "Secrets of Successful Muslim Wives" for all married sisters.
- "Say It With Love: Communicate, Connect & Cure Conflict" for all married sisters.
- "Love Scripts: Getting Through To Him" for all married sisters.

- “Newlywed Nuggets: Golden Marriage Advice” for newlywed wives.
- “Choosing Your Other Half: Marriage Tips for Muslim Singles” for single brothers and sisters.

She has produced free courses for sisters on fasting, umrah, and marriage. Find them on her website.

www.muslimacoaching.com
IG: @muslima_coaching FB: @muslimacoaching

Recommended Readings

1. A Muslim Woman's Guide To Menstruation Rulings
https://inspiredmuslimwomen.com/muslim-woman-menstruation-guide/

2. How the Prophet ﷺ Treated Menstruating Women
https://www.muslimacoaching.com/how-the-prophet-treated-menstruating-women/

3. Istihada: What Is It With Examples
https://www.muslimacoaching.com/istihada-what-is-it/

4. IUD & Istihada
https://www.muslimacoaching.com/iud-coil-spotting-ruling-of-blood/

5. The Excused Person's Rulings: A Complete Breakdown
https://www.muslimacoaching.com/the-excused-person-rulings/

6. How to Pray With Istihada
https://www.muslimacoaching.com/how-to-pray-with-istihada/

7. Praying While Sitting During Pregnancy
https://www.muslimacoaching.com/can-pregnant-women-pray-sitting-down/

8. Five Must-Know Rulings For Praying During Labor
https://www.muslimacoaching.com/five-must-know-rulings-for-praying-during-labor/

9. The Sick Person's Prayer With Pictures
https://www.muslimacoaching.com/the-sick-person-prayer-with-pictures/

10. Menstruation Rulings Related to Ramadan
https://www.muslimacoaching.com/menstruation-rulings-during-ramadan/

11. Worship In Ramadan for a Menstruating Woman
https://www.muslimacoaching.com/worship-in-ramadan-for-a-menstruating-woman/

12. Taking Medication To Delay Menstruation in Ramadan
https://www.muslimacoaching.com/is-it-permissible-to-take-medication-to-stop-your-menstrual-flow-during-ramadan/

13. Maliki Position on Touching & Reciting the Qur'an
https://www.muslimacoaching.com/maliki-position-on-touching-reciting-quran/

14. Umra Rites During Menstruation
https://www.muslimacoaching.com/performing-umrah-while-menstruating/

15. Umra Advice and Answers for Menstruating Women
https://www.muslimacoaching.com/advice-answers-for-menstruating-women/

16. Medication to Block Menstrual Blood During Umra
https://www.muslimacoaching.com/medicine-to-stop-menstrual-blood/

17. More Menstruation Articles for Free
https://www.muslimacoaching.com/category/menstruation-issues/

SCAN THE QR CODE TO ACCESS THE ARTICLES

Bibliography

ʿĀbidīn, ʿAlāʾ ad-Dīn. *Al-Hadīya al-ʿAlāʾīya*

al-Indarpatī, ʿĀlim ibn al-ʿAlāʾ. *Al-Fatāwā at-Tātārkhānīya*

al-Kāsānī, ʿAlāʾ ad-Dīn Abū Bakr. *Badāʾiʿ aṣ-Ṣanāʾiʿ fī Tartīb Al-Sharāʾiʿ*

al-Marghīnānī, Burhān ad-Dīn Abī al-Ḥasan Alī ibn Abī Bakr. *Al-Hidāya* with commentary by al-ʿAlāma ʿAbdil Ḥayy al-Laknawī

al-Mawṣilī, ʿAbdullāh ibn Maḥmūd. *Al-Ikhtiyār li Taʿlīl al-Mukhtār*

al-Maydānī, ʿAbd al-Ghanī al-Ghunaymī. *Al-Lubāb fī Sharḥ al-Kitāb*

al-Qārī, Mullā ʿAlī ibn Sulṭān Muḥammad. *Fatḥ Bāb al-ʿInāya bi Sharḥ Kitāb al-Nuqāya*

- *Mirqāt al-Mafātīḥ Sharḥ Mishkāt al-Maṣābīḥ*

al-Shaybānī, Muḥammad ibn al-Ḥasan. *al-Aṣl*

al-Shurunbulālī, Ḥasan ibn ʿAmmār. *Marāqī al-Falāh Sharḥ Nūr al-Iyḍāh*

al-Ṭaḥṭāwī, Aḥmad ibn Muhammad. *Ḥāshiyat al-Ṭaḥṭāwi ʿalā Marāqī al-Falāh*

Burhanpuri, Nizam along with a group of scholars. *Al-Fatāwā al-Hindīya*

Ibn ʿĀbidīn, Muḥammad Amīn. *Manhāl al-Wāridīn min Bihār al-Fayḍ ʿala Dhukr al-Mutaʾahilīn fī Masāʾil al-Ḥayḍ*

- *Radd al-Muḥtār ʿalā al-Durr al-Mukhtār*

Ibn Māza, Burhān ad-Dīn Mahmūd ibn Aḥmad. *Al-Muḥīṭ al-Burhānī fī al-Fiqh al-Nuʿmānī*

Shaykhī Zādah, ʿAbdur Raḥmān ibn Muḥammad. *Majmaʿ al-Anhur fī Sharḥ Multaqā al-Abḥur*

Printed in Great Britain
by Amazon

42510060R00059